WHAT PEOPLE ARE SAYING

"I was pleased to work with Lynn Jones as her Graduate Advisor in our Christian Counseling program. In this capacity, I had the opportunity to witness firsthand Lynn's strong love for the Lord as well as His Word and His Holy Spirit. She is passionate in her pursuit of the things of God and thorough in her prayerful application of His revelation to her life. I heartily recommend Lynn and her ministry to you!"

Dr. Charity Kayembe
Christian Leadership University

My name is Brenda McGuire. I am a realtor, piano teacher, and a former 4th grade school teacher. I am very honored to encourage my dear friend, Lynn Jones. She is a godly example of a faithful Christian lady. She loves her family with a pure heart and also loves serving Jesus and helping people. Lynn is an uplifting author. She treasures writing her books and sharing God's Word to encourage fellow believers and lead lost souls to Jesus.

Lynn Jones is a teacher of God's Word and has focused on helping people discover their potential for greatness regardless of their circumstances. She is a powerful prayer partner and cherishes the Presence of God. Lynn's love for Jesus permeates in everything she does, making her inspirational to us all!

Reverend Jo McGuffin
Executive Director, Zoe Healing Center / Edmond Healing Rooms

I met Lynn Jones at Aglow International Oklahoma City, Oklahoma, Lighthouse around two years ago. She came to speak to our group and to give her testimony as portrayed in her first book ***CONFESSIONS OF A BLONDE***. Shortly after, she was invited to serve on the Aglow OKC Lighthouse Board. She is an inspirational speaker with great insight for what the Body of Christ needs. Lynn has contributed greatly to our group in her passion to connect with people. I look forward to reading and learning from her new book. May God continue to bless her in all of her endeavors.

Linda Curtiss, President
Aglow International Oklahoma City Lighthouse

I have known Lynn Jones about eight years. She is by far one of the most colorful and interesting people in my life! Then, when I thought I knew her fairly well, I read her book ***CONFESSIONS OF A BLONDE***. So delightful! Full of valuable stories, lessons and anecdotes from her life. I so enjoyed reading it and was sorry to come to the end.

Thea Carlson Reust, nurse and friend

I have known Lynn for several years. The first time I met her I knew that she would be used of God to change the world! Lynn is a pure hearted woman of God, a woman in a mission to share the love of Jesus and His faithfulness with all she meets. As you begin to read her story through her first book, ***CONFESSIONS OF A BLONDE***, as well as her new book, ***SOAKING MOMENTS WITH LYNN***, ask your Father to reveal his love to you. Let Him touch your heart!

Jeanne Linville
Sunshine Ministries

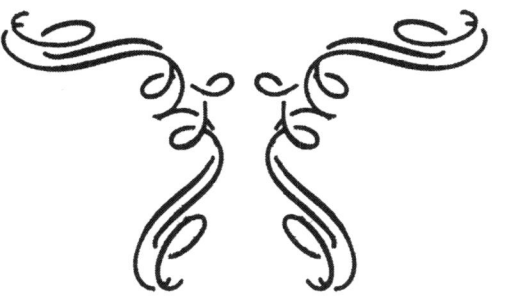

DEDICATION

I am dedicating ***SOAKING MOMENTS WITH LYNN*** to my readers, those I have had the privilege to meet and speak to through church gatherings, Christian Women's Club and Aglow, Bible studies I have led, on Facebook, or speaking to as a friend or enjoying a gathering with several friends to celebrate a precious moment or event. In addition, this book is dedicated to those who adhere to Isaiah 55:1. To those adherents, "Come, all you who are thirsty, come to the waters, and you who have no money, come, buy and eat! Come, buy wine and milk without money and without cost" and also from Revelation 22:17, "The Spirit and the bride say, 'Come!' Let the one who is thirsty come, and let the one who wishes take the free gift of the water of life." I believe the scripture I have included quite liberally will speak to all who want to go deeper in the Spirit and soak in His Presence.

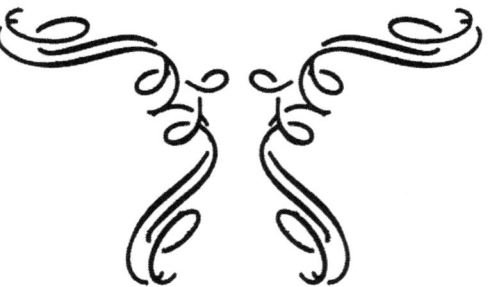

TABLE OF CONTENTS

Just For Fun

Postscript

ACKNOWLEDGMENTS

I am grateful to my husband, Michael, who has encouraged me to continue on this pursuit of following my dream of inspiring others. I am thankful for the technical support that he has given me likewise. Thank you Honey for being a dream builder in my life.

Thank you, Harriet Ford, for your assistance in editing my book. It has been wonderful knowing you since our teaching days together. You are an inspiration and a very fine mentor to me.

Thank you Penny Burt for your cover illustration and graphic designs. We have been friends for many years! I am grateful for your friendship and it has been marvelous seeing how the Lord has worked in your life on so many levels.

Thank you Eric J Burt and Father's Heart Productions for publishing my book and the use of your poem, "Waterfall of His Life". I am trusting great doors of opportunity are opening for you and Penny.

I am grateful to all my children, Grace, Patrick, Kenneth, Adam, son in-law John, daughter in-law Kyla, grandchildren, Gloria, Mikey, Caleb, and baby Hazel for enriching my life in so many ways. I love you all!

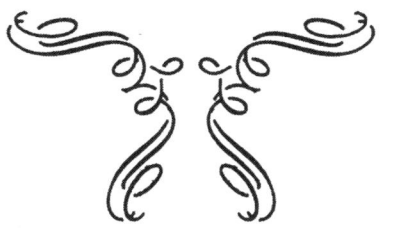

INTRODUCTION - WHY I WROTE

SOAKING MOMENTS WITH LYNN

Through the years, I have been learning the value of long periods of contemplation in prayer, listening to praise or soaking music which is a place of great intimacy with the Lord, or writing down thoughts and prayers unto the Lord. These are all outlets for me to draw nearer to the Presence of the Lord and it has been my desire to gather as many people with me on this journey of love and growth in the Lord. I want to be challenged in my Christian walk and I believe there are many others that want to also. It is definitely a death to self and being alive to the Holy Spirit in a multitudinous of ways.

The Christian walk is an adventure and I believe that others as well as myself want to be used in many fruitful ways through God's grace. I trust this book will allow people who read it to have the freedom to ask themselves questions about going deeper in communion with the Lord and as a result come to know Him in fresh, vibrant, joy-filled ways. It is not about being perfect. Jesus became the perfect sacrifice for us on the cross and therefore has enabled all of us to receive His perfect gift of grace and salvation to walk in freedom, hope and love.

Please allow yourself to put soft music on if you like when you read these articles and answer these questions. I believe the Lord has a word for each person who "has eyes to see and ears to hear." That is His desire for each of us. As Psalm 34:8 says, "Taste and see that the Lord is good!" God loves you and so do I! Be blessed!!!

YOU WANT THIS BOOK IF…

You want to grow and are unafraid to confront yourself with nagging questions you want to find answers for. It may also be for a small group study where you can read the articles, grapple with the questions together and thereby find answers together. There are some elements of fun too and my prayer is that Christians find they can be happy, followers of Jesus and share this happiness with others encapsulated in salvation that Jesus made available to each of us. I look forward to hearing how the Lord has enabled each of you, my readers, to gain more victory, peace and joy in your life through these experiences. I pray for you! Be blessed!!!

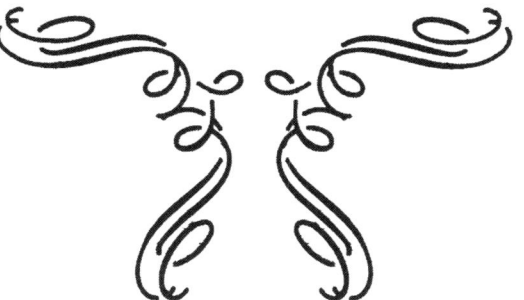

WATERFALL OF HIS LIFE

God's life is like a river,
flowing next to a cliff.
And we are empty pools,
waiting below all dry and stiff.
And the only thing preventing us
from being filled to the rim
are blockades of dirt and rocks,
our natural dams of sin.
The mighty rush of water
erodes the soil some,
but the breakthrough won't occur
'till the salvation plan is done.
Then the awesome power of Jesus
will blast away our paths,
sending forth His gracious life,
pouring into thirsty baths.
And these pools will fill and fill
'till we overflow and try
to breakthrough the dams below us
where other people are dry.
It is a continual process,
a waterfall of sorts.
But we always must remember
that God's river is our source.

Psalm 36:7-9
John 7:37-39

By Eric J. Burt
www.fathersheartpoetry.com

THE MANY MEANINGS OF WATERFALLS

From a variety of sources, I have happily discovered the many hidden symbolisms and features of waterfalls. From a prophetic perspective, waterfalls are representative of the Holy Spirit with great power. Waters that came from salt water were rooted in a contaminated, spiritual environment. It is optimal that the salt water converts to pure or fresh water. In this analogy of water, the river of God leading to the waterfall possesses fleshly activities and demonic doctrines. The length of the run depicts geographic world wide conditions as well as being time-wise or covering several centuries. What ungodly ideas and activities which have continued that are firmly entrenched and epitomize human traditions and/or aberrant doctrine have to give way to new, pure spiritual life birthed in fresh, pure water. The Holy Spirit takes us from saltwater to freshwater and a new baptism of power for those who are being equipped for spiritual warfare. The new floodgates open up a "prophetic trail."

The waterfall also represents unleashed creativity in a constant fluid shape that is ever changing and renewing. In addition, openness, flexibility, and spirituality are revealed. Revelation is another characteristic of the waterfall.

In literature, the waterfall is a symbol of change and is often present at turning points in the story. They are mostly a sign of life, but when murky waters appear, it can also be seen as a sign of death. For the Christian person, death to self is a noble and necessary goal to become more Christlike in all we do and say. In classical Chinese tradition, waterfalls manifest a symbol of impermanence; it persists but never in the same way.

In the Judeo-Christian tradition, there is an insistence of intentions, an invitation to delight, and to be an observer of revelation. A great release of emotion, rejuvenation and renewal of spirit are also included as well as a continuous flow of the ebb and flow of creation.

Waterfalls are unharnessed motion. They can be a symbol of application to our lives in areas we need to master and control for our own spiritual benefit. There is a permanence of form despite a change of content.

In another dream I researched, the waterfall was "tamed" by man creating a concrete staircase for the waterfall's descending. Man ruined the natural beauty for control and money. Men ended up destroying what they wanted to preserve. The waterfall is God's Spirit. It is awesome in power, spectacular and unpredictable. The staircase represents man trying to control things for himself and not trusting the awesome power of God in the waterfall that can be destructive and so sometimes generates fear. However, when we try to reroute God's power, we end up losing power. Some scripture references were given such as John 3:8, Mark 7:13, and Psalm 46: 3-4. The first scripture shares, "The wind blows whenever it pleases. You hear its sound, but you, cannot tell where it comes from or where it is going. So it is with everyone born of the Spirit." Showing a parallel with man's attempt to control things, the verse in Mark instructs, "Thus you nullify the word of God by your tradition that you have handed down... In the passage from Psalm 46, we clearly see and hear the waterfall - "though its waters roar and foam and the mountains quake with their surging. There is a river whose streams make glad the city of God, the holy place where the Most High dwells." The latter surely showcases the purity which we aspire to attain.

I also found there is a connection with God's grace being equated like standing beneath a waterfall. God's disposition toward us is one of continual grace even if upon looking up, we see nothing but more water coming down on us. Lamentations 3:21-25 references the steadfast love of the Lord never ceases and His mercies never come to an end. We need to soak in God's goodness and seek refreshment in Him. Even challenging and difficult circumstances are God's gifts to us. Psalm 42:6,7 is a beautiful picture of a waterfall. "My soul is cast down within me; therefore, I remember you...deep calls to deep at the roar of your waterfalls, all our breakers and waves have gone over me."

There is no doubt the Lord often speaks loudly to us in the waterfall to get our attention to comply with His deepest purposes for our lives. Will we hearken to His messages for us and indeed soak in His Presence? I hope so!

www.angelfire.com/inHisName/waterfall:htm
vaughanhoystudio.com/blog/2013
www.heavennet.net /visions/rivers-waterfalls.htm
sb2.org/gods-gracelike-standingbeneatha-waterfall

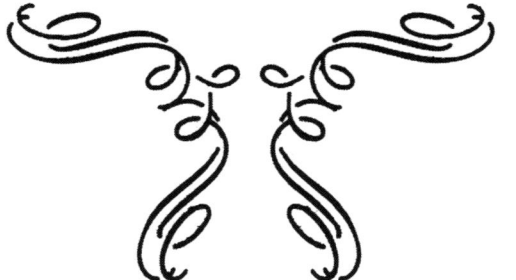

CHAPTER 1 - ARE YOU A BLESSING?

I am happy to share some of my meditations with my readers that reflect what I like to say is fresh manna from my perceptions of the heart of God. As we grow in our relationship with the Lord, it is not enough to have simply head knowledge of the Bible and theology, but we need to have a healthy heart attitude.

Do you know what the heart of man thinks? Proverbs 23:7 tells us, "As a man thinks in his heart, so is he." Understanding the role of the heart in our relationship is crucial, I believe, to true intimacy with the Lord and immense emotional and spiritual health. When this understanding is in place, then the realization of the healing of the heart is an ongoing process. This is good! It keeps our dependence on the Lord and our heart in a humble posture so we are in an expectant, receiving mode!

Join me now in our exploration of various heart issues in the form of my personal meditations and many references to the Word of God. I am excited about what impartations of God's Holy Spirit (or as some say Holy Spirit because He is a real, active Person Who lives inside believers) show you as you read and meditate by immersion in the Scriptures or what thoughts these words may provoke or excite in you.

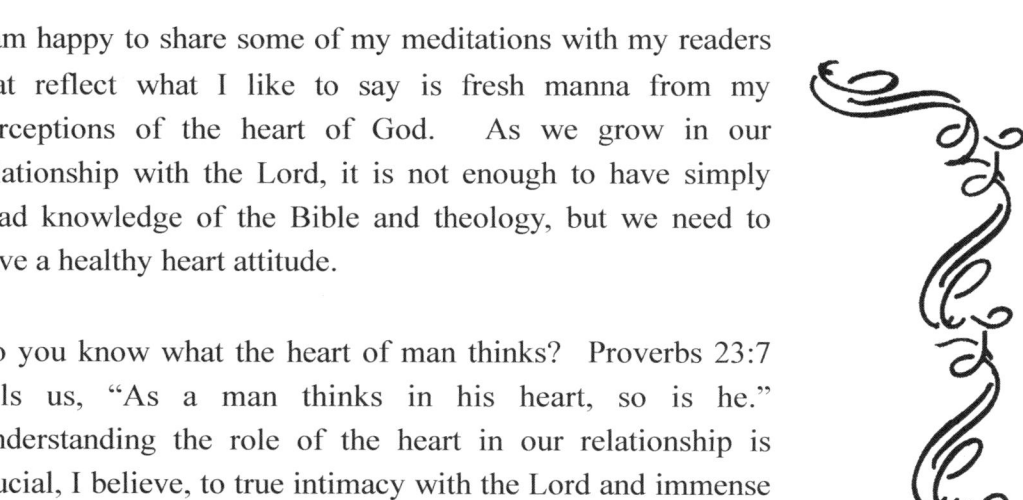

In the book ***IDOL LIES***, by Dee Brestin, she maintains there are innermost desires we have which seek to displace and replace God. These types of desires are not our friends, but are instead enemies. Attitudes and acquisitions the world and even the church world applauds such as power/control, affirmation, safety/security can actually be idols, Dee suggests. When this happens, we are wrapped up in ourselves rather than seeking to serve or bless others.

In my life, I have needed to have a paradigm shift in my thinking in order to have a better grasp on what actually brings more peace and happiness in life. Jesus said in Matthew 23:11, "the greatest among you will be your servant." This is not merely theory, Jesus asserts, but is the way to attain everything our heart desires. What an assertion!

Two examples of servants in the Bible are Moses and Joseph. Moses was called the meekest man in the world. Meekness is actually strength under control. Imagine a person such as Moses who had the privilege of being raised in Pharaoh's palace as a prince of Egypt, then killed an Egyptian and was promptly ostracized from the high society he was accustomed to. After meandering in the desert for a time, Moses meets Jethro, priest of Midian, and is thrust into the role of a shepherd for 40 years. The Egyptians hated this occupation. It was as lowly as you can imagine, but Moses yielded to this new role and learned obedience, the Word tells us. He was humbled in this endeavor to the degree that the Lord was able to talk to him through a burning bush, and he wouldn't pass it by, but observed the Lord's interaction with him.

Through his experience of shepherding sheep for 40 years, Yahweh directed him to be the deliverer of His people of about 2.5 million. Moses was broken in spirit through this sojourn in the desert in order for the Lord to pour out His glory and birth deliverance through Moses. What a blessing he was.

Then we have Joseph who naively shared his dream with his brothers about shafts of wheat grain. The brothers and even his father were represented, bowing down to the shaft in the middle represented by Joseph. There was understandably some indignation that the brothers and even father Jacob demonstrated towards Joseph. The brothers were so inflamed with jealousy that they hatched a plan of selling Joseph as a slave to nomad marauders. They then dipped Joseph's beautiful, multi-colored coat his father had given him into goat's blood. They shared their sorry story to Jacob who overcome with grief, ripped his own coat thinking with the evidence shown to him that Joseph, his most beloved son, was now dead.

Joseph learned to serve when he himself could have succumbed to extreme grief and self-pity. Joseph's brothers sold him into slavery, but Joseph proved what a faithful servant he was to Potiphar in the land of his captivity, Egypt. He was put in charge of all Potiphar's household until his encounter with Potiphar's wife. Potiphar's wife desired Joseph, but when he refused her, she betrayed him and lied about his intentions towards her. Then Joseph was thrown into prison, but again he served and was in charge of the prisoners. He was able to give helpful counsel to the butler, who was released, but it wouldn't be for another two years that Joseph would be freed. When prompted by memory of Joseph after Pharaoh had a dream about which he could not make heads or tails, the butler remembered Joseph had a talent. Joseph was awarded for his God-given skill of understanding and interpreting the dream by being made second in command to Pharaoh himself.

The lesson is there may seem to be repeated episodes of disappointments over lost expectations, dreams or adventures, but in the process, we are gaining strength, tenacity and endurance. These qualities cannot be ascertained lightly, but are usually forged through the furnaces of afflictions of all kinds.

Then Joseph was thrown into prison, but again he served and was in charge of the prisoners. He was able to give helpful counsel to the butler, who was released, but it wouldn't be for another two years, Joseph would be freed. The butler finally remembered Joseph and his interpretation of the butler's dream. When he was prompted by memory of Joseph after Pharaoh had a dream he could not make heads or tails of, Joseph was released from prison when the butler remembered

Joseph had a talent. Joseph was awarded for his God-given skill by being made second in command to Pharaoh himself.

When the Lord asks us to be servants, it is for life! First of all, we need to keep in mind that He is our exceeding great reward (Genesis 15:1). This point was made early in our Bible knowledge and understanding to underscore the number one priority the Lord wants to be in our lives. This will help us in the long run as we learn to cultivate patience and serve with right motives. When the rewards come in this life, they are actually bonuses or icing on the cake as we have already set our sights on the Lord. To be a servant is to be a blessing to others. There is no other kind of life I would rather live.

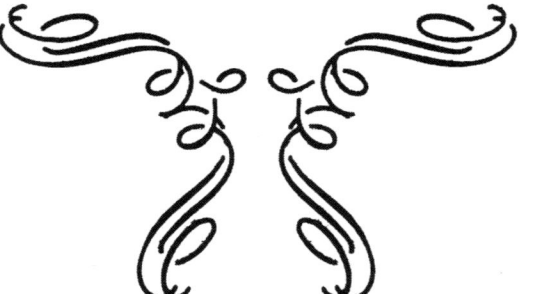

CHAPTER 1 – ARE YOU A BLESSING?

1. What is your definition of spiritual manna? Give a personal example and an accompanying scripture. Mine is my mini blog of Blessed by His Presence. Choose from 15 verses about manna – knowing Jesus online such as Exodus 16:31. It says: “The house of Israel named it manna, and it was like coriander seed, white, and its taste was like wafers with honey.

2. What does it mean to be expectant and receiving? Expectancy can be strengthened through diligent searching of openings, passing the word around with friends, or acting on a Word from the Lord, either from the Bible or from an impression He gives that lines up with the Bible. The Lord’s opportunity may come in a form you may not be looking for, but receive the opportunity, however small, because with the right attitude, greater opportunities can be accelerated.

3. Give an example of being wrapped up in ourselves and how it results in the works of the flesh. Give an example of serving or blessing others.

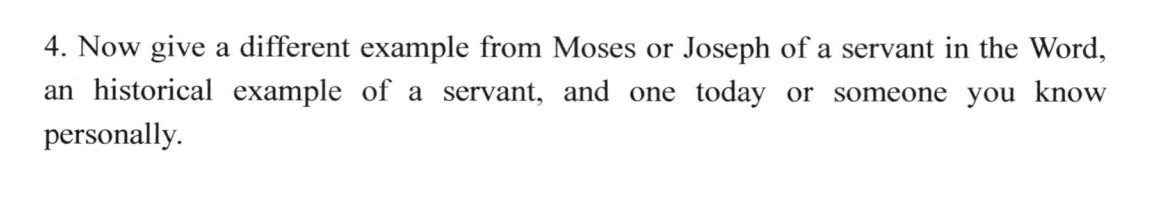

4. Now give a different example from Moses or Joseph of a servant in the Word, an historical example of a servant, and one today or someone you know personally.

5. How is the Lord chiseling you, or in other words, how is your flesh being mortified or crucified? What is a difficult task the Lord has asked you to do?

6. What gives you peace, where does your anointing lie, or what are you being drawn to? For me, speaking, writing, and counseling/ministry are my top three.

7. Give an example of God's favor in your life and a scripture on favor.

8. Do the same for thankfulness and what are you particularly thankful for?

9. Name a trial where you have had to maintain a good attitude? Give a scripture on good attitudes (Phil 2:1-30, I Peter 3:13, Matthew 6:33, Ephesians 4:4-6, Ephesians 3:6, Romans 5:1-21, Ps 45:7 to name a few) and be prepared to explain what it means to you. Search online for Bible verses on Positive Attitudes.

10. Can you name a reward the Lord has given to you? Use a scripture mentioning heavenly rewards such as James 1:12, Rev 22:12, II Timothy 2:11-12, Romans 11:19-22, Matthew 25:21, or I Corinthians 3:8 for starters.

CHAPTER 2 - CELEBRITY GOD

The idea of celebrityhood, I believe, is what drives our culture that has lost its way. What is the definition of a celebrity? According to Wikipedia, a celebrity is a person who has a prominent profile in day-to-day media, and because of this, commands some degree of public fascination and influence. A celebrity is usually expected to be wealthy, but not always. He is commonly denoted with fame and fortune implied with great popular appeal, prominence in a particular field, and is easily recognized by the general public.

Often being a celebrity is attractive because we think it will offer us our soul's deepest desires and wants. As we age and have not perhaps achieved that notoriety, we can be tempted to think we really missed it.

Everyone can be a celebrity if he wants to. It's easy through a digital camera and videotaping about anything you want and can post it. It reminds me of 1 Corinthians 6:12. It says, "all things are permissible, but not all things are advantageous or beneficial." Also in Romans 14:16 we are told, "Therefore, do not let your good be spoken of as evil." How do these verses go together and apply to the culture we live in today?

We often find ourselves in a quandary since we know Christ has made us free to do good works. In fact, Colossians 2:16, 18 tells us we are "not to judge in food or in drink, or regarding a festival or a new moon or Sabbaths" and "let no one cheat you of your reward, taking delight in false humility, and worship of angels, intruding into those things which he has not seen, vainly puffed up by his fleshly mind."

Have we gone to the other side of the spectrum when it seems we crave attention and even desire worship at almost any cost? It seems we will stoop to extreme flaunting or compromise of our values in order to achieve that goal of self-adulation. Is this the best way to use our liberty? Some individuals or churches have tried to combat this by going back under the law.

Galatians 3:1 warns us, "O foolish Galatians, who has bewitched you that you should not obey the truth"…and Galatians 3:3, "Are you so foolish? Having begun in the Spirit, are now being made perfect in the flesh?" Also, Galatians 3:2b queries, "Did you receive the Spirit by the works of the law or by the hearing of faith?"

We know the answer is not legalism as these verses point out, but then how do we find freedom and worth? This, I believe, is what drives our culture. The deception is because we live in such a fast-paced society, we can easily get lost in the shuffle. We erroneously believe if we don't get on this endless merry-go-round of fame, fortune and success, we will be left behind, ignored or forgotten. That may be true if our goals are as fleeting as these. If our goals are temporary, our rewards, satisfaction and fulfillment are also woefully temporary. If we are on that merry-go-round, it is akin to going around that proverbial mountain.

This means satisfaction or fulfillment can only be attained through achieving that next goal, that next picture or video which shows our best features or the love or adulation from others. Perhaps this is why we elevate celebrities so much. We want what we imagine they have which is truly an illusion. Who is the celebrity we can follow hard after (Psalm 42:1 beckons "as the deer panteth for the water, so my soul pants after You,") and can show us the way to liberty? Galatians 5:13 reasons, "For you brethren, have been called to liberty, only do not use liberty as an opportunity for the flesh, but through love serve one another."

This is the type of celebrity we can get behind. Our Father God is worthy of all praise and honor. Revelation 5:12 proclaims: "Worthy is the Lamb who was slain, to receive power and riches and wisdom and strength and honor and glory and blessing." He is an unselfish God who calls us co-heirs (Ephesians 3:6 "…should be fellow heirs of the same body, and partakers of His promise in Christ through the Gospel") with Him. Most importantly, God's love for us is all encompassing and far reaching.

His forgiveness is displayed such as our sins being separated from us as far as the east is from the west, found in Psalm 103:12. The only condition is to believe in such a wonderful God Who shows us how to truly have the fulfillment, satisfaction and love we all crave. Celebrities? The only true One is nearer to us as than the breath we breathe. "In Him we live and move and have our being" (Acts 17:28). He is that "Friend who sticketh closer than a brother (Proverbs 18:24)."

Clearly, our God is what an authentic celebrity is about! As we recognize this, we will "humble ourselves and He will exalt or promote us in due time" (James 4:10). This honestly is what life should be about! Let's go for it.

CHAPTER 2 - CELEBRITY GOD

1. Have you ever wanted to be a celebrity? Why or why not? How has God made you to stand out? Read Psalm 139 for clarification if you have any doubts how God feels about you.

2. Give an example or two about what is permissible, but not advantageous in your life. Please explain and give scriptures if possible.

3. Where have you craved attention? How can you use the redemption of that misplaced focus to bring liberty to yourself and others? There is a difference between the God-given desire to use our talents and the lust that can sometimes accompany them!

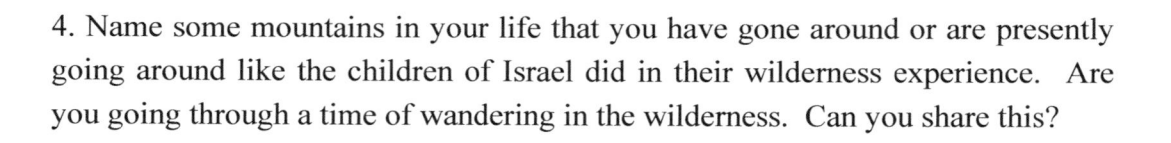

4. Name some mountains in your life that you have gone around or are presently going around like the children of Israel did in their wilderness experience. Are you going through a time of wandering in the wilderness. Can you share this?

5. Who is someone who may be a celebrity you may admire? How can you edify this person in a godly manner by writing a letter, committing to a cause of mutual interest by taking action, sending money, sharing on Facebook or praying for?

6. Now, what are some tangible ways you can serve another through your participation in their activities, social causes, issues, practical ways you can be a blessing?

7. What are some character areas the Lord has been working on in your life lately to bring you closer to recognizing you are a co-heir in Christ?

CHAPTER 3 - YOUR BUSYNESS SPEAKS SO LOUDLY I CANNOT HEAR YOU!

How often do we say, "I'm busy," in response to any question we may be asked in the course of a day? This simple response can speak volumes – we are trying to impress, justify our actions, don't want to engage in intimate conversation, or even making an attempt to demean our interrogator. Not only can we respond verbally in this insipid, passive manner but even more disastrously, our very own lives can reveal these types of answers and even more.

Sometimes it is not how much we are able to do, but what are we actually called to do. This is not often easy to discern, but we can have indicators from being anxious, irritable, clenching fists, rapid palpitation of our heart and other negative emotions or bodily responses to give us some clues.

The question we should ask is not how busy we are, but are we fruit-bearing or productive in our lives? When we are producing fruit in our lives, our attitudes are different and our priorities will shift. No more is it about how we can impress others, but looking for ways to bless others. We no longer are looking for ways to busy ourselves with non-essentials, but with what brings true beauty and glory to God. This takes being led by the Spirit, and being sensitive to His ever-present nudgings.

Somehow we think the Lord will overlook us if we do not draw undue attention to ourselves; therefore, we stay inordinately busy in an effort to say to Him, "Look at me! Here I am! Can't you see what I have been doing for you?" We become a little bit like Martha in Luke 10:38-42. Martha may have wanted attention when she asked Jesus to make sure her sister Mary would help her and essentially see what she was doing. When we're at this place, we more than likely have a faulty perspective about our identity. If we truly understood we are complete in Jesus and His love, we would not be searching for substitutes.

It is also a matter of what or who we want to reflect in our lives. If we are only interested in our personal reputations or prestige, then that is what we will reflect. If we have eternal values, then our desire will be to reflect our Eternal Master, Savior and Friend, Jesus Christ.

Our busyness, interestingly enough, often reflects what god or gods we are actually serving. James 4:1-3 laments, "Where do wars and fights come from among you? Do they not come from your desires for pleasure that war in your members? You lust and do not have. You murder and covet and cannot obtain. You fight and war. Yet you do not have because you do not ask. You ask amiss, that you may spend it on your pleasures." What is our busyness often wrapped up in? Our pleasures, not our serving! The lack of acquisition of our pleasures is what causes so much rotten fruit in our lives and in some cases sickness, disease, or even death. The motivation for our busyness is a rather important matter, don't you think?

When our sights are set "on things above not on earth" (Colossians 3:2), our peace, joy, and true productivity factor will go up. We will face challenges and trials as sure as the sun rises and shines, but as James 1:1-2 emotes, "we are to count it all joy when we encounter various trials…" This is what debilitates so many of us in this faith journey. Our focus is on the wrong emphasis and we can therefore "faint and lose heart" (Galatians 6:9). Our goal needs to continue to press through those areas in our lives that can so defeat and warp our visage. We should not be busy just to fill in time or cover those areas that need to be treated and healed. When we have relational fruit-producing productivity, we are happier and are more equipped to terminate all which would steal our precious time for God ordained assignments. Do I think we might be able to hear one another more clearly and with greater understanding if we practice these principles? Emphatically yes.

We all need to be heard – so let's practice on one another and not let our busyness create deafness in our conversation! We live in a world that is full of ways we can promote ourselves! It is the antithesis of what I Peter 5:6 tells us which is, "Humble yourselves, therefore under God's mighty hand, that He may lift you up in due time." I think it is due time which can cause us the most unrest. It is easy to second-guess or even berate ourselves for not seeing signs along the way that would help further us along the pathway to success. Perhaps it is our idea of success that needs resolving.

CHAPTER 3 – "YOUR BUSYNESS SPEAKS SO LOUDLY I CANNOT HEAR YOU"

1. Enumerate or list some areas when you say "I'm busy". What does this list say about your motivations?

2. How can you distinguish between what you are called to do and not called to do? How does your body talk to you as mentioned in the article? In the areas where you are busy, where do you experience peace? This will be where your fruitful productivity is!

3. What are some substitutes in our lives for God's Presence? Or in other words, where are we trying to get attention or be noticed? Read Luke 10:38-42 again to get a fresh perspective on how Martha tried to be noticed instead of rest in the Lord's Presence.

4. Name what you like to do for fun or pleasure. When could it possibly turn into an idol to which James 4:1-3 speaks? How could you turn some of those pleasures into acts of service? Be creative as you imagine possibly engaging in these acts of service!

5. Have you ever been burned out? This is another way of describing Galatians 6:9. How? How can you arrive at some deeper inner and emotional healing so you won't stay stuck or hooked in some behavior pattern? Who do you need to forgive? What do you need to repent from?

6. Has your idea of success changed over the years since you have become a Christian? How has it changed and what is true success to you? Please feel free to include scripture that would support your new discovery!

7. What are some obstacles and challenges in your life? Is your foundation in the Lord sturdy enough to sustain you? (Read Matthew 7:24-27 about the wise and foolish builders.) Give some scriptural reasons why you believe this and what have been some concrete results?

8. Give a modern day example or one in history of the kind of difficulties Joseph faced. How has their story inspired you? You can share an article or read an excerpt from a book to illustrate your reasons for choosing this person.

9.What are some rewards God has given you in this life? What would some examples be of rewards based on I Corinthians 3:10-14 which would merit the Lord's blessing in heaven? Which actions in your life would not?

10. What new area is the Lord calling you to be fruitful in?

CHAPTER 4 - ALWAYS A CONFERENCE ATTENDEE, SELDOM A SPEAKER

We've all heard the adage, "Always a bridesmaid, never a bride." I think this same phrase can be applied to anything in our lives we may enjoy, but find ourselves in a rut and not seeing the progress we desire. Perhaps it is our perspective that is problematic. Sometimes we can look at such experiences as wilderness experiences or perhaps we can see them as the Lord's way of protecting us from a faulty objective or it is simply additional training that we may need. Wilderness experiences are indeed times of strengthening! Just look at Abraham's lifetime of training until he was 100 to have his son Isaac, Moses' 40 years of training, Joseph's almost 20 years of training as a slave and imprisonment, and Paul's 14 years in the desert of Arabia before the Lord released him to preach. Our own Lord, Jesus Christ, only started his ministry at the age of 30 and then had a ministry for three years. Being human, we do have human expectations, desires and fears regarding what we think we should be accomplishing.

The Lord knows the way we should go and like Paul in Acts 26:14 we should not attempt to kick against the goads. The word goad is used: 1) for such instruments as spurs, scourges or nails and 2) to describe torments or enticements. When we are frustrated or perplexed about some of the routes our lives have taken, if we probe further than is wise or safe to, I believe, we can fall into the trap of kicking against the goads.

For Paul, this statement was referring to the "futility of persecuting the church." (Stanley D Toussaint in Bible Knowledge Commentary 1988, p.429).

It is so easy to kick against the goads or the spurs which can keep us on the right track. Because of our limited understanding, we don't know the way we should take, but the Lord does. Here is where the joy of the Lord can develop and blossom. When we develop in trusting in the Lord, even when there seems to be repeated episodes of disappointments over lost expectations, dreams or adventures, we are gaining strength, tenacity and endurance. These qualities cannot be ascertained lightly, but usually forged through the furnaces of affliction of all kinds.

In my life, it often seems in turning over every unturned stone, volunteering to serve at events, taking various classes some with certificates, some not, volunteering and attending conferences, my own experiences as a speaker and seller of books has been a trickle and not extensive.

I know there is still much chiseling which is ongoing. I am learning to be thankful in all things, not promote myself, but be open to where I can contribute and go through those doors the Lord will open. Even if I am often overlooked or it would seem, I can take heart the Lord will promote me in due time as I keep myself under His humbling hand.

Humility can take various forms. It is important to mark our motives. If I have to ask myself why I am doing a certain task or get a check in my spirit about an undertaking, I need to take notice of this. Conversely, if I am sensing a drawing of my spirit towards a particular pursuit and receive the blessing of peace, I can be confident of the Lord's leading. This should be my gauge so even if an activity, conference or potential speaking event seems to call out to me, if it does not come with the accompanying peace or invitation of the Holy Spirit, it is not something in which I should engage.

Then I can have peace I have made the right decision, don't need to second-guess or berate myself, in spite of what appearances may dictate. This can also dispel the tendency to be defensive and having to have my own way. This can only work when we start training ourselves to follow after the spirit, not what is culturally acceptable, or pleasing to the flesh.

So, can I be happy or content in God's timing even when it seems like I am being overlooked? Yes, I can be because "He has made everything beautiful in His time." Everything we are able to do is a gift from God, so as Colossians 3:23 (NLT) urges: "Work willingly at whatever you do, as though you were working for the Lord, rather than people."

Even today as I pondered areas I was not happy about, I saw a picture in my mind's eye. It was a picture of a large smile and I immediately recognized it as the smile of God. This smile has been able to offer a deep sense of peace, fulfillment and satisfaction that eclipses any other false contender. When we have the knowledge of the Lord's favor in our life, nothing else can compare. It has the ability of soothing fear, removing sorrow, inspiring hope and confidence and giving momentum where it is needed. In fact, as I meditate on another stone of offense in my life, the Lord reminds me of a great truth. When I feel I am not adequate for gathering everything I have built my life on to validate my sense of importance or give credence to my abilities or talents, the Lord reminds me of this significant scripture in 1 Corinthians 3:11. It says "no one can lay any foundation other than the one already laid which is Jesus Christ."

This means when I am tempted to berate myself or compare with another because I am viewing my inadequacies or when I am tempted to praise myself, I cannot build on those faulty foundations. Perhaps the Lord wants me to be more firmly grounded on this truth before He opens other doors of blessing.

What is your foundation built on? Can it sustain you during your times of repetitions, perceived loss and being overlooked? It takes courage, character, and a desire to be conformed into God's image and not our own. The Lord will see us through as we keep "His smile" uppermost in our hearts and minds. It is not in our striving that we can have the desires for which we aspire.

It is in our yielding! When we are tempted to lament our perceived obstacles, being ignored, or overlooked, we can sit back and bask in God's Presence and His smile. Another way scripture tells us to overcome is by the blood of the Lamb and by the word of our testimony. This is how we can wait joyfully on Him, as we are the perennial bridesmaid and not a bride, the conference attendee and not the speaker. Has this been a blessing? I hope so!

CHAPTER 4 – ALWAYS A CONFERENCE ATTENDEE, SELDOM A SPEAKER

1. Can you identify a wilderness experience in your life? How did it eventually strengthen you in your life's journey?

2. What are 2-3 of your stepping stone experiences and how have they brought you closer to your goals?

3. Can you name a time when you have been at a crossroads between choosing to go in a direction that would please the Lord or please people? Give an example of each.

4.. Identify a faulty foundation you have built your life upon. How did you learn from this exercise?

5. When has there been a season or time in your life where you have felt God's smile resting upon you?

CHAPTER 5 - IT IS NEVER TOO LATE TO GO AFTER YOUR DREAMS

Despite all the Lord has done for each of us, we all know we have unfulfilled expectations and dreams not coming to fruition. It is easy to become downcast and disillusioned especially when we try approaching those dreams from different angles.

One example of going after dreams, in the case of healing, is mentioned in connection with the children's bread. This was first a concept used in the telling of the story of the Canaanite woman in Matthew 15:21-28. She asked the Lord to have mercy as her daughter was demon-possessed and suffered terribly. The disciples wanted Jesus to send her away, for she kept crying out. Jesus answered her by saying that He was sent only to the lost sheep of Israel. He also said. "It is not right to take the children's bread and toss it to the dogs." This Canaanite woman responded with such faith when she said, "Yes, even the dogs eat the crumbs that fall from their master's table." Jesus startles everyone involved watching this scene, by saying, "Woman, you have great faith. Your request is granted. And her daughter was healed at that moment."

There is an attitude we can learn about from this woman. She let nothing deter or distract her from believing not only that Jesus could heal her, but also she was counting on His great compassion. It appears she knew the Lord's heart. She didn't allow her race, a Canaanite rather than a Jew, dissuade her. She was the wrong gender, and she was not intimidated over the clamor the disciples expressed because of her shouts for help. What an example for today's men and women. We truly need to know the character of Jesus in order to have the courage of our convictions in order to move forward in our faith.

Is it as easy as knowing the Lord's character and count on our healing? I believe the answer is both yes and no. John 14:14 appeals to us, " If any of you ask anything in My Name, I will do it." If this is the case, why at times have we not seen more instantaneous miracles such as we saw with the Canaanite woman? Second Corinthians 1:20 relates in the NLT, "For all of God's promises have been fulfilled in Christ with a resounding Yes." And through Christ, our Amen (which means yes) ascends to God for His glory. Romans 8:31 acknowledges in the NIV, "What then, shall we say in response to these things? If God is for us, who can be against us?" Again, if this is the case, then the trouble is most likely, in our receiving. This is not to bring condemnation, but instead these verses on God's will for us, should significantly inspire us!

We may have more hindrances in the time we live in, but we also have more helps. Let's analyze and dissect this truth a little bit. There is so much progress being made in the area of neuroscience. Dr. Caroline Leaf is a person who is acquainted with this science. She tells us: "Research has shown thinking deeply until an understanding is reached leads to improved physical changes in the brain." Stress is the body's reaction to toxic choices, which result from toxic thought circuits." Dr. Leaf stipulates that 87%-95% of illnesses that plague us today are a direct result of our thought life. What we think about affects us physically and emotionally. It is an epidemic of toxic emotions, she says. For more illuminating thoughts, refer to www.drleaf.com.

In spiritual terms, progress has also been made. We are understanding better that "we wrestle not against flesh and blood, but against principalities, powers, rulers of the darkness of this world, and against spiritual wickedness in high places" (Ephesians 6:12). There are many ministries and churches that understand the role that demonic possession or oppression can play in a person's life. Jesus did defeat satan at the cross especially as He said, "It is finished." Just like salvation needs to be received as well as the baptism of the Holy Spirit, the benefits of salvation need to be applied.

Why have we been told that "satan is as a roaring lion seeking whom he may devour" (I Peter 5:8) if this were not so. We are not to be naive so "that no advantage would be taken of us by satan, for we are not ignorant of his devices" (II Corinthians 2:11). We are also to be sober-minded and vigilant, so that we are not lulled to sleep by this world's system or the enemy. If we take a superior attitude regarding spiritual matters, we will not only miss the blessings the Lord has for us, but also can unwittingly open the door for the enemy of our souls.

What about in the areas of changing a career such as Jan Karon, beloved author of the Mitford Series, did at around the age of 50. I remember still seeing her beautiful face on the cover of **GUIDEPOSTS** several years ago and being so inspired by her story. She had been in the advertising business and made the radical change to write novels. Ms. Karon came to know the Lord later in life at the age of 42 and her writing does indeed reflect her faith.

The series she authored takes place in an idyllic town reminiscent of those from her North Carolina upbringing. The series chronicles the life of Father Tim Cavanaugh, an Episcopalian priest, and the people in the town of Mitford with whom he interacts.

Ms. Karon has written over ten books and encountered opposition first from herself as she strove to find the idea for her book and then two more years facing rejection from publishers. She is definitely an example of one pursuing a life-long dream of becoming a novelist from an early age. Jan says working in the advertising business developed a strict discipline which she transferred over to her skills as an author.

What dreams are below the surface still needing attaining and accomplishing? In the case of changing a career, it is important to learn our callings. This can help propel us into the momentum we need to develop for stamina, endurance and perseverance.

The jet stream which we often associate with airplanes is the same idea we need to adopt when accentuating our dreams and goals. What is a jet stream? It is the fast, flowing, narrow air currents found in the atmosphere.

It is interesting to note jet streams typically have a meandering path taking on shapes that can start, stop, split into two or more parts, combine into one stream, or flow in various directions including the opposite directions of most of the jet. This tells me something! Even though some may take a direct route to attain their direction, most of us take the routes that actual jet streams take. We can think we have reached the pinnacle of success if we match this type of classification, but in truth all the routes use parts of the jet stream. Who knows what your jet stream calling might be? (https://en.m.wikipedia.org/wiki/jetstream)

Faith is required in both cases, whether it has to do with healing of any kind, in a change of careers, finances, relationships, and so forth. The Canaanite woman would not be deterred by the rejection of her race and even gender. Jan Karon was not deterred either. Healing still is the children's bread! I don't know about you, but I don't want to miss out on this tremendous benefit of Zoë salvation. Zoe is truly the fulfillment of dreams. It has to do with real and genuine life, a life active and vigorous, devoted to God, blessed abundantly, even in this world of those who put their trust in Christ, but afterwards the resurrection to be consummated by new accessions (among them a more perfect body). The Canaanite woman was looking towards this! How about you? What dreams are beckoning to you?

According to Ephesians 2:6 (NIV), "God raised us up with Christ and seated us with him in the heavenly realms in Christ Jesus." Psalm 27:5 says, "For in the day of trouble he will keep me safe in His dwelling, He will hide me in the shelter of His sacred tent and set me high upon a rock."

This is the important thing - we are seated in heavenly places with the Lord! Following the Lord's jet stream for our lives is the greatest joy we can find for living and for following after our dreams!

CHAPTER 5 – IT'S NEVER TOO LATE TO GO AFTER YOUR DREAMS

1. What are some unfulfilled dreams and expectations you have? What are some pro-active actions you can take to accomplish those goals?

2. What like the Canaanite woman in Matthew 15:21-28, could deter you from overcoming obstacles in your pursuit of your dreams? In the Canaanite woman's case, she was the wrong ethnic group (not a Jew) as well as the wrong gender (not a man) for that day.

3. What gives your stress? Refer to Dr. Caroline Leaf's website, www.drleaf.com and mention a thought or two about how our thought life can affect us emotionally and physically.

4. Can you give an example in your own life when your faulty, toxic thinking brought about sickness in your life? Someone else you know? How can it be circumvented in the future?

5. How can you be more vigilant in your life in your prayer time, relationships, areas of social awareness, money management?

CHAPTER 6 - WHAT THE WORLD NEEDS NOW IS THE PRESENCE OF GOD!

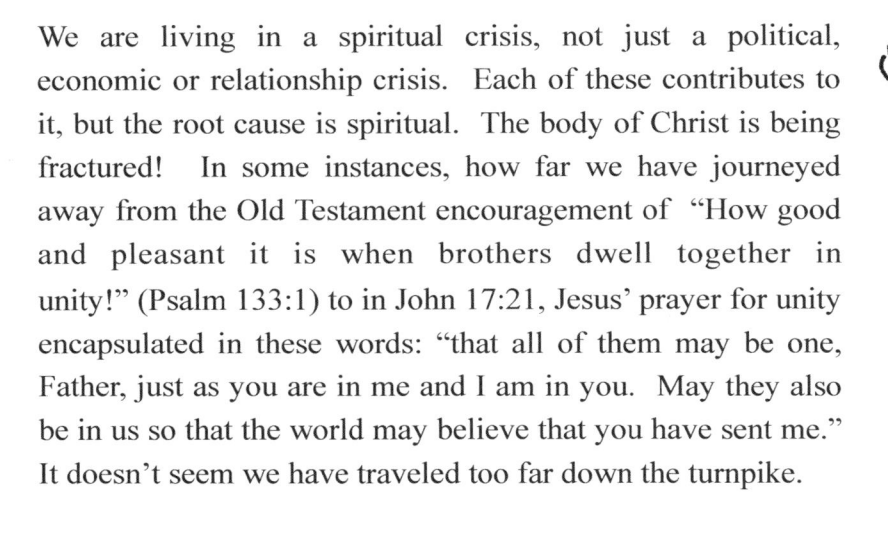

We are living in a spiritual crisis, not just a political, economic or relationship crisis. Each of these contributes to it, but the root cause is spiritual. The body of Christ is being fractured! In some instances, how far we have journeyed away from the Old Testament encouragement of "How good and pleasant it is when brothers dwell together in unity!" (Psalm 133:1) to in John 17:21, Jesus' prayer for unity encapsulated in these words: "that all of them may be one, Father, just as you are in me and I am in you. May they also be in us so that the world may believe that you have sent me." It doesn't seem we have traveled too far down the turnpike.

With so many attempts many churches have pursued, why is there even more splinter groups than ever before? There is an overwhelming good side to this, but let's look at the downside first. What seems to happen to us, is we discover a hidden or lost truth and we decide to camp out there. Not only this, we often end up worshipping this truth to the neglect of many other truths.

This fallacy stirs up those of other religious idols or fruit of the flesh. James 3:16 teaches (NIV), "For where you have envy and selfish ambition, there you find disorder and every evil practice." Why are splinter groups called such a name? Internal splintering and fracturing occur which cause hurts and pain. If left unchecked, this will spill over into messy divisions within a group, denominations or the corporate body of Christ. What starts out as a blessing, uncovering lost truths and/or wrong motives can result in poor or tainted objectives. We were made to worship, but let's make sure it is the true God and not the gods of our own creation, which definitely includes pet doctrines and legalistic bondages we place on others and ourselves.

Denominationalism, as one favorite evangelist opined, is the symptom of a dysfunctional family that being in this case the body of Christ. It is amazing how insidious the enemy is and how he can bring just subtle changes into our thoughts and demeanor when speaking to or about someone else who is in another denomination. It is time to check our snide attitudes when they first appear. It takes place inside our innermost being and rises up just like a serpent or a cobra that is coming out of the basket. In places where there are snake charmers, music is played and gently the crafty serpent makes his appearance. This kind of poisonous siren sound that we hear from our culture tries to pervade the atmosphere in church and has an influence that has stealthily been winding its way like a snake through the crevices, crooks and crannies of our lives.

Okay, what is the overwhelming good side? When we seek the Presence of God, He will lead us into all facets of His Character. When we desire to know Him more than to cling to our opinions, our interpretations of theology, the gifts He dispenses, our talents, or anything that could serve as a distraction to true intimacy with the Lord, we are onto something. The baptism or the fire of the Holy Spirit has been such a unifying agent for the body of Christ! It is the Holy Spirit Who has single-handedly made quick work of denominational rancor, elitism, selfishness and barriers to believers and non-believers who desperately want to have the Presence of God in their lives.

When we use lost truths as aids or tools to get a clearer view of the Holy Spirit and His Presence, we may be approaching the right track of answering Christ's prayer that we as the body of Christ will be in unity even as He and the entire Godhead are in unity as illustrated in John 17. The dictionary definition of unity is the state of being in full agreement. In art or literature, it is a combination or ordering of parts in a literary or artistic production that constitutes a whole or promotes an undivided total effect. There is also a consistency in style and character. Wow! As the body and bride of Christ, if this can indeed be said about us, what else really matters? We will be the reflection of God's Presence in the world and without the aforementioned barriers, the Lord will more freely and unrestrictedly flow not only in our services, but in the marketplace, schools, hospitals, government, the arts, foreign mission fields, and in our families.

I am looking for His Presence to come and overshadow me today. What about you?

CHAPTER 6 - WHAT THE WORLD NEEDS NOW IS THE PRESENCE OF GOD

1. Name a couple of lost truths which have been uncovered, sometimes have led to splintering, but show how they can be redeemed to bring unity to the body of Christ. For example, some denominations think baptism is necessary for salvation, yet Romans 10:9 says, “if you confess with your mouth Jesus is Lord and believe in your heart that God raised Him from the dead, you will be saved.“ Knowing scripture can bring unity!

2. Where are there areas in your community where you can link arms together with another denomination and support a work they are doing? For example, the Catholic Church has spearheaded the 40 Days of Life campaign by having marches and vigils as we commemorate the rights of the unborn.

3. How has a recognition of the Holy Spirit's baptism of fire helped your character, your love walk, and operating in the spiritual gifts with the aid of the fruit of the Spirit?

4. What are some ways you practice the Presence of God in your life? What are your quiet times like?

CHAPTER 7 - IT IS TIME TO TAKE A BATH

As I contemplated what I was going to write on, I meditated how we are living in a time in which it is very hard to discern cleanliness and purity. It is as if what we are surveying in our society are very muddy waters in all aspects of life. While meditating on this, I tuned into a Oral Roberts University Chapel worship service. It is nicely televised on Oral Roberts University's local station. The next song that was being sung was on the blood of Jesus that washes me white as snow. Can the Lord meet you in an instant, when in my case, I want confirmation on the next article to be written? I think He does meet us at every junction.

In my meditation, I am seeing such a time we are living in where the wheat and the tares are growing up together (Matthew 13: 24-50). In this parable, the wheat and tares (weeds) grow up together and we are admonished by the Lord to not uproot or pull up the wheat prematurely. This would be harmful. We live in a day in which it is more difficult to differentiate between the two. Because of this, it does seem like the cultural waters of society have become more sullied, dirty, unattractive, and gives offensive spiritual odors.

I have made some interesting observations about wheat that very well do tie into the Christian life. First of all, wheat doesn't have a deep root system. If we are thinking only about growth, we may not think this would be such a good thing. After all, don't we want to grow deep in the knowledge, counsel and admonition of the Lord? This particular analogy has to do according to a sermon I read with the shortness of the root system because we are not to be so easily attached to the things of this world. In fact, the wheat grows up very high with this short root system as if for reaching initially for heaven's boundaries. Secondly, the wheat grows and ripens, bears fruit and quickly passes away. This is like the Christian's life. We don't stay on this earth for very long. We have been commissioned after we gain our salvation to go out and make disciples of all men. The manifest destiny of this mandate is our fruit. We do not dare waste the time the Lord has given us for our assignment. As the wheat grows higher than the root system, it reminds us of "setting our affections on things that are heavenly, not the things of this world." Also, as the wheat grows high, the head of the wheat actually bows down which should show us that humility is needed as we attain more success in our lives.

The tares are infiltrators into the church who may or may not know they are counterfeits or false brethren as 2 Corinthians 11:26 points out. The elderly evangelist, Billy Graham, said among the saved in his crusades, 70% were church members. As the sermon also indicates, the tares can become wheat. One thing that characterizes a tare is the object of their salvation or what is a person trusting in?

Okay, what does this have to do with taking a spiritual bath? Very simple! Those things we trust in other than the Lord no matter how good it may seem (our righteousness) is actually filthy rags as Isaiah 64: 6 proposes. Then if we don't recognize our unclean state and proceed by wallowing in the mud as the prodigal son did, we meet the conditions for the need of taking a spiritual bath. Actually this is true for all of us in various degrees. When Jesus told Peter He needed to wash His feet or He would not have any part of Him, Peter countered by saying then wash all of me; however, Jesus said it was only necessary for the feet to be washed. In John 13:10a, Jesus insists, "Those who have had a bath need only to wash their feet; their whole body is clean." This could also be interpreted by saying when we come to the Lord for salvation, our whole being becomes clean, although walking in the world every day indicates a need for daily cleansing from the cultural and internal debris every day which accosts us.

When we become more service-minded and less self-absorbed or have a sense of entitlement, we become more mindful about what it means to be cleansed spiritually and have a sense of God's purity, satisfaction, resolution and fulfillment in our lives. Matthew 23:11 tells us, "The greatest among you will be your servant." By living in a more humble manner, we seek the welfare of others and find a need we can fill. This is the abundant life that John 10:10 speaks about.

We are in a time in which we are seeing those who are tares have reaped the blessings of God because of the diligence, character and foundational principles of others. The tares instead of thanking the Lord for His blessings have seen those blessings as what they have done and they are living for themselves. Because there has been such a rich godly heritage into which the godly have sown, the fruit of such a heritage has supported the tares as well as the wheat. This is why the waters have become murky and everything about life has become less identifiable with true Judeo-Christian principles. Psalm 107:2 is a solution to this modern day conundrum on how we should live. It says: "Let the redeemed of the Lord say so, whom he hath redeemed from the hand of the enemy." Also, Psalm 11:3 tells us, "When the foundations are being destroyed, what can the righteous do?"

It is time to get back to our righteous foundations found in the Word of God and follow His plan for our life. In this way, we will be assured we are following the right path. Psalm 51 gives us also a remedy. Without a cleansing of the heart, we will feel dirty, disheveled, and filthy because of our sin. Let's trust the Lord's cleansing stream in our lives and go out into the world and offer others an opportunity to see clearly and know the beauty that is in our relationship with the Lord!

CHAPTER 7 - IT IS TIME TO TAKE A BATH

1. Give an example of what is a fruit producing work (wheat) and a work that has the appearance of a good work but does not produce fruit (tares). For a pro-life position, crisis pregnancy centers which seek to spare life and abortion clinics that give the semblance they offer aid for the mother, but actually encourage the killing of the unborn child and leaves devastating consequences on the mother is applicable.

2. What is an example in your life of setting your affections on things above and not of this world? How can you be pro-active in promoting the area in which the Lord has called you to engage?

3. Can you give an example from your own life as to what your filthy rags might be? Are you willing to discard them for the Lord's robe of righteousness? This is alluding to Isaiah 61:10. Mention a verse and action you are willing to apply for this transformation to transpire!

4. Give some examples where the foundations have been destroyed in our political and governmental system, in the medical world, education, and in how we relate to one another.

CHAPTER 8 - LET'S TAP INTO THE LORD'S SUPERNATURAL

There is a lot of confusion in these days. It is certainly in the world we live in today, but even more egregious is that terrible inconsistencies and differences exist in the body of Christ. You might say there are factions, theological cliques, and acute disputes among God's people. That should not be!

So why is this true? This isn't an easy answer. When we press into wanting more of God's Presence, it has to be more than an intellectual pursuit. Some, though, in the body, stop at this point as if this was the overall goal. It is helpful for the purposes of understanding the Greek and Hebrew derivation of biblical words that certainly deepen and enhance our appreciation for the Word of God. Is this, however, sufficient for allowing us to enter into the Presence of God? No, because we are told we must worship the Lord in spirit and truth. John 4:24 enthusiastically asserts, "God is spirit, and His worshipers must worship in spirit and in truth."

The predicament is what is worshipping in spirit? Many groups of Christians often equate the spirit with lofty thoughts found in God's Word, but it is so much more than this. I believe it is part of what the Word says are signs and wonders. We are to follow the Lord, not signs and wonders according to 2 Thessalonians 2:9, but signs and wonders are to follow believers according to Mark 16:17-18. This is a major area of confusion. I get it! Christians don't want to fall into deception and therefore shut down any moving of the Spirit whatsoever. They would rather play it safe than step out in faith for the Lord and have the Lord permeate His being throughout their lives to live supernaturally.

In some cases, there is more emphasis on the letter of the law. Galatians 5:1-3 spells this out rather clearly for us. In this passage, the Paul chastises the Galatian believers by calling them bewitched. He then proceeds to ask, "Did you receive this Spirit by the works of the law, or by believing what you heard?" He equates this by beginning in the Spirit, and now trying to finish by means of the flesh. That should provoke a wake up call in all of us and signify that the Word cognitively received only is not sufficient. The Lord wants to speak to us in our hearts. Some may call this an unction or anointing.

One description given of unction is that "wherever the Holy Spirit touches a man's heart it diffuses itself through his whole soul, and makes him wholly a new creature…makes the conscience tender…brings the secret, mysterious, and invisible, yet powerful anointing oil of grace into the heart; it receives the truth as from God, and truth thus coming from God penetrates into the soul" (www.gracegems.org/Philpot/unction of the Holy Spirit).

The same could be said about a similar word, anointing, in which we are advised that the anointing flows through us when God's heart touches another person's heart through your heart and in other words, the anointing of the Holy Spirit is the Holy Spirit of Jesus (www.seekgod.org/message/anointing.html). He flows as a river of love, from the throne of grace, through the hearts of believers, bringing life to all that receive His touch.

It comes down like our entire Christian life, to a matter of choice when it comes to accepting more supernatural intervention in our lives. This is a major source of excitement and joy when I know I have this freedom and am not forced to be a carrier of the Holy Spirit and His working in my life. According to the passage in Romans 8:10-17, we who are children of God are led by the Spirit of God. The Spirit we received brings about our adoption and sonship.

According to Romans 8:17, if we are children then we are heirs of God and co-heirs with Christ. As children and heirs, we can trust the Lord to bless us not curse us. Furthermore, Luke 11:13 (NIV) says, "If you then, though you are evil, know how to give good gifts to your children, how much more will your Father in Heaven give the Holy Spirit to those who ask Him." We can trust the Lord wanting to love us and manifest or reveal Himself more fully and transparently to us than we are wanting to receive.

Can this confusion finally be dispelled and expelled from our churches, but most importantly, our hearts? I believe this is part of the joy of letting the King of Glory enter in! We are on the verge of seeing this King of Glory's return!

CHAPTER 8 -LET'S TAP INTO THE LORD'S SUPERNATURAL

1. What does worshipping the Lord in spirit and truth according to John 4:24 mean to you?

2. Give an example of some biblical truth in the New Age movement or even the occult that has been hijacked for evil purposes in which the Lord wants to redeem. An example is a psychic who tells a person about aspects of the person's life they couldn't know but interaction with demons could bring forth this knowledge. Some one who operates with the gift of the word of knowledge knows something through God revealing what is edifying and gives God the glory.

3. What are signs and wonders? Have you had the experience of signs and wonders following you?

4. Have you started something in God's grace, but end up finishing under bondage or in your own strength?

5. Find a verse about the unction of the Holy Spirit and the anointing of the Holy Spirit and describe what each mean to you.

6. What is your understanding of the baptism of the Holy Spirit? Give verses to support your conclusions?

CHAPTER 9 - THE VALUE OF STANDING IN FAITH

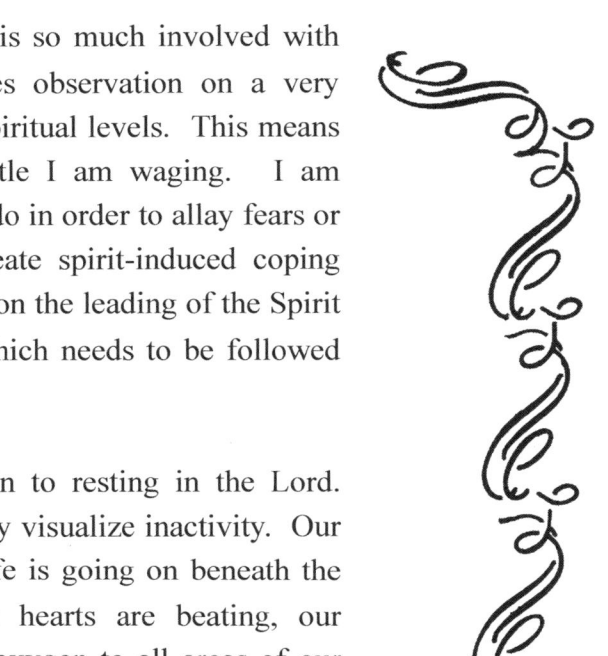

Standing is not inactivity! There is so much involved with this process of faith! It requires observation on a very heightened level of practical and spiritual levels. This means I am not in denial about the battle I am waging. I am watching for practical things I can do in order to allay fears or prevent prolonging of pain or create spirit-induced coping mechanisms. It is important to act on the leading of the Spirit or impressions one might sense which needs to be followed through by action.

Standing in faith is a close cousin to resting in the Lord. When we rest physically, we usually visualize inactivity. Our bodies aren't moving, but much life is going on beneath the surface to keep us alive. Our hearts are beating, our bloodstream is bringing food and oxygen to all areas of our body, keeping our organs functioning as well as taking away waste that would contaminate our body. It is also a time when our brain is not inactive too. We dream and as believers, we know the Lord can speak to us in this manner. We are told in Psalm 37:7, "Rest in the Lord and wait patiently for Him. Do not fret because of him who prospers in his way. Because of the man who carries out wicked schemes."

Spiritual warfare goes or must go on for the desired result to become reality. This is where the two, standing in faith and resting in the Lord, come together. In order to rest, we must stand against the onslaught of the enemy. We have to be grounded in truth in order to be effective against three major enemies – the devil, the world, and the flesh. These three are no match for the Lord Who stands unparalleled in every way above all others. We are in a safe place when we stand with Him. Since we are standing in Him, we can therefore rest in Him, claiming victory peacefully which only He can give. It is a mighty position to be in and not to be considered lightly.

Sometimes we may ask the question, when do I know I have done all, and when I should stand? What comes before that phrase in Ephesians 6:13 is, "Therefore take up the whole armor of God that you may be able to withstand in the evil day and having done all, to stand firm."

Let's go over briefly what the armor of God is. It is found in Ephesians 6:13-18. We are told to put on the belt of truth so we need to know how to discern between what is falsehood and what is truth. We need the breastplate of righteousness and should not compromise or dilute what the Lord says is right. Our feet should be shod with the preparation of the gospel of peace. We should be peacemakers according to Hebrews 12:14 which says, "Make every effort to be at peace with all men and to be holy; without holiness no one will see the Lord." This action takes much diligence and patience. It should be practiced daily!

As we become fully persuaded as Abraham was in believing that God had the power to do what He promised us in Romans 4:21, (NIV), then we have the confidence to know the Lord has heard our petitions. This can help when we are tempted to waver in faith. We know according to James 1:6, "one who doubts is like a wave of the sea blown and tossed by the wind." It truly seems to be our attitudes of heart and mind that is severely tested by the enemy of our souls. This is also how we overcome as we rehearse what the Lord has done for us, His promises and answered prayer in the face of major challenges and trials.

Is it worth it to stand in faith day by day? The Lord does give us supernatural ability to have peace and joy, as we stand in faith. Consider the alternative - be discouraged if we flag in faith. That can give way to all manner of negative emotions, not the least of which is despair. For what do we want to be known? What should our legacy be? Could there be a connection between one who stands in faith and the Lord saying, "Well done, good and faithful servant." My faith educated guess is an unqualified yes!

CHAPTER 9 - THE VALUE OF STANDING IN FAITH

1. Where have you needed to stand in faith? Give verses that will help give you a secure footing and support your experience.

2. Resting in the Lord is also like having peace when you don't see positive outcomes, but trust God. Where do you need peace right now and can you remember when the Lord has given you peace in difficulties?

3. How have you had to wage spiritual warfare in your life or on behalf of another? Name a part of the armor the Lord has strengthened you in and where you are presently weak.

4. Our goal is to become fully persuaded as Abraham was in every area of our lives that God is at work. What can help you with this goal? Share verses in the areas you need persuasion.

CHAPTER 10 - GOD'S WAYS ARE NOT OUR WAYS AND THANK GOD THEY'RE NOT!

How often do we try to manipulate God to do things we want in our lives? We may not realize that is what we are doing. It's almost like we think we are capable of helping God along with His program of completing what He started (Philippians 1:5). When you look at it this way, it is quite shocking and even repulsive that we would think this way. Isn't He the Alpha and Omega, the Beginning and the End, and doesn't He make "all things beautiful in His time" (Ecclesiastes 3:11)? Why do we take this approach so often of coercion and debating with the Lord about His ways?

We say we want fuller, richer, freer lives and for some reason, we have a problem trusting God. We seem to be much more practiced in listening to the lies of the enemy who adeptly counterfeits the truth of God. We need to discipline ourselves. I Kings 8:58 excitedly shares "that he may incline our hearts to Him, to walk in all His ways, and to keep His commandments, His statutes, and His rule, which He commanded our fathers." Such rich, beautiful words, but what do they mean for us?

I think it means we are to become thoroughly acquainted with Him with Whom we have to do. The Word says in James 4:8, "Draw near to me and I will draw near to you." We can so often intellectualize or reason what this actually means. Developing a love for God's Word is a wonderful way to do what the Word instructs us to do in following hard after the Lord. Matthew 11:30 reminds us, "My yoke is easy, and my burden is light." I think this can refer to applying God's Word to our lives. What a blessing to know we don't live this life unequipped, without power to live it effectively, or the love that is so essential through the sacrifice of Jesus!

This in turn develops into a strong hunger to keep on going and plummet into the vast richness and refreshing of God's ways and His thoughts. By choosing to travel along this pathway, we cannot be blinded to the enemy's devices. He does not want us to make progress in our walk with the Lord. Many distractions are thrown in our direction and the enemy's ploy is to get our attention off the Lord and on to the problem or idols in our lives. If he can help to cause disappointment, fear, or despair, he can capture us at his will. It is our job as believers to understand how to undermine the enemy.

The Lord has given us many tools, and has raised up people in the fivefold ministry such as apostle, prophet, evangelist, pastor and teacher in order to accomplish the task of defeating the enemy. We are also given spiritual gifts (1 Corinthians 12:1-11). They are given for the common good, such as manifestations of the Spirit through a message of wisdom, a message or word of knowledge, of faith, gifts of healing, miracles, prophecy, speaking in different kinds of tongues, and interpreting tongues. There are additional practical gifts found in Romans 12:6-8. These entail prophecy as mentioned before: exhorting, showing mercy, service, administration, giving, and teaching. How wonderful when all these gifts are in operation! The enemy doesn't stand a chance when we come together as the body of Christ and operate as one.

CHAPTER 10 -GOD'S WAYS ARE NOT OUR WAYS AND THANK GOD THEY'RE NOT

1. What is an area you honestly don't understand about the Word in which you would want to debate the Lord on? What is your conclusion at this time?

2. What yoke are you unnecessarily shouldering? Give verses like 1 Peter 5:7 which says, "Cast your care upon the Lord, for He cares for you" to remind you that the Lord is our burden bearer.

3. What is a distraction or an idol in your life right now that needs a God-given strategy to overcome? Name an action to take and a verse to support your action.

4. You may not be one of the fivefold ministry groups, but where do your gifts lean? Are you one who gathers and builds things (an apostle), like to tell people about Jesus (evangelist), are a nurturer, counselor (pastor), likes to inform or instruct (teacher), or are musical (praise and worship)? Give reasons and scriptures to support your thoughts.

5. What are some gifts and talents you have that can be used for the glory of the Lord?

CHAPTER 11 - PRAYER CHANGES EVERYTHING!

Is this really true we may ask? It is akin to getting into our secret place with God (Psalm 91:1) that honors the Lord by saying, "He who dwells in the shelter of the Almighty shall abide or rest in the shadow of the Almighty. I will say of the Lord, He is my refuge and my fortress, my God, in whom I will trust."

Everyone likes good secrets! Why are we often so loathe entering into the secret place with God if that is the case? I think it is much like the comparisons we make with one another because we don't really believe the Lord has a tremendous plan for our lives. We don't honestly believe our spending quality and quantity time with the Lord is more important, adventurous and exciting than anything else we could do. I think that is the place we need to come to and that only happens through spending time in prayer! The grass-is-greener-on- the-other-side can apply to spiritual matters, also.

If we could nip in the bud, the tendency to think if we just had certain attributes, breaks, gifts, and talents as someone else, we would be in the place we should be. That is self-deception which is included in the following verses: I John 1:8, Psalm 36:1-4, Jeremiah 2:34-35, Jeremiah 17:9-10, Revelation 3:17, Matthew 23:13-15, Luke 11:42-52, John 8:33-34, James 1:22-26, James 4:13-16, Jeremiah 5:31, Jeremiah 6:13-14. I could go on, but will stop here with this last verse. Boy, I saw this in a new light! The Lord says, "From the least of them to the greatest of them, everyone is greedy for gain and from the prophet to the priest, everyone deals falsely. They have healed the brokenness of my people superficially, saying peace, peace, but there is no peace!"

Greedy for gain doesn't just mean monetary. It can be for status, position, recognition, popularity, respect and the like. How humbling to be rebuked by this scripture and ones similar to it. Self-deception should be avoided like the plague and I think that is the reason there are so many verses on this topic.

Meditation is a form of prayer. Joshua 1:8 says, "This Book of the Law shall not depart out of thy mouth, but thou shalt meditate therein, day and night that thou mayest do all or observe to do all that is written in it. Then you will be prosperous and successful." Meditating is likened to chewing the cud, digesting, bringing it back up and ruminating again and again on the goodness of the Lord. This form of prayer needs to be applied generously through our daily diets. As a result of this discipline, the Lord is being abundantly doused into every area of our lives. We will know the way we should go, the thoughts we should have, the joy the Lord wants us to have, the awareness regarding the battle we are in and our ability to put on the whole armor of God.

A scripture that may give us a sneak preview about what happens during prayer is this one in Jeremiah 1:12 saying: "The Lord watches over His Word to perform it." Prayer in conjunction with the Word of God yields tremendous benefits. There are several definitions for the word "watch." Here are a few that can help in our understanding of prayer. They include to be attentive or vigilant, to keep guard, to keep someone or something under close observation, be expectant, to take care of, to be on the alert. When all these aspects of watching are in motion, we can get the impression that there is nothing outside the Lord's reach or understanding. Performing His Word is an action.

To perform means: to carry out, accomplish, fulfill a task or function, to do something to a specified standard. This last definition is particularly intriguing to me because it shows order, purpose and direction. This truly can be associated with prayer. Because of even a clarified understanding of this scripture, we can be assured that since we are being watched over, our Lord is bringing to our remembrance His Word for answers to prayer. He is causing circumstances to move in our favor since our confession is lining up with God's Word.

Dire events don't have to dissolve us into a heap of despair and ruin because we know the Lord has the bigger picture since He can see the end from the beginning. Wow! What a perspective to have! When we are praying in a manner not lining up with God's Word, we will receive a check in our spirit which is an inner knowing that all is not right.

You and I are responsible as believers to follow the light we have been given in God's Word and turn away from a wrong course of action or speech. This is another word for repentance and is applicable for every person. The non-Christian needs to follow and cultivate the measure of faith (Romans 12:3) that is given as the Lord is wooing him to salvation. To turn away, after the Gospel has been clearly explained and communicated is the same as hardening one's heart. The Lord cannot hear prayer because the prayers are in accordance with what man feels or believes about himself, rather than what God says is the correct way to move forward. This again is applicable to all of us. James 4:3 demonstrates, "You ask and do not receive because you ask wrongly, to spend it on your passions."

Is God speaking to us? I would say loudly and clearly, even though ironically He prefers to speak in a still voice (I Kings 19:11-13). He wants to prevent wrong results in our lives, but if we live ignorantly or have willful rebellion, He will use adverse circumstances and events to get our attention! Can prayer change our attitudes so we are in a much better position to hear Him and act in accordance with His Word? Yes, this is the area where I believe He most fervently and consistently works in our lives. He wants to move us from a place in which we are looking away from what can benefit us, to what can fulfill and bring life to others.

What stunts our believing? Often, it is because we don't think our prayers are being heard or perhaps we are not thankful for how the Lord is answering us. Prayer and thankfulness do seem to go together. We are encouraged to "give thanks in everything for this is the will of God concerning you" (I Thessalonians 5:18). I know I need to take mega doses of thankfulness in my life. It is easy to be tempted by the distractions in life, but I do believe as I draw closer to the Lord, His ways will prevail and I will see an increase of more koinonia, amongst God's people. It will be in attitudes of helpfulness, unselfishness, giving, serving and most importantly, worship and praise to Our Creator, Savior and Lover of our souls.

It is time to believe God for great things in the Spirit realm! What has the Lord laid on your heart to believe for? Are there unsaved and deceived loved ones for which you don't see much hope? Don't fret! Trust the Lord to change their atmospheres from those of doubting, mocking and unbelief to a flourishing life giving faith in the Lord.

Can the Lord provide the finances you need when you only have, metaphorically speaking, two fish and five loaves of bread? Trust Him to show you where the hidden manna of provision is being placed. Help us not to miss those opportunities, lest like the physical manna the Lord gave His people in the wilderness, it spoiled and is unable to be used, for the opportunity has passed on by.

Healing of bodies, mind, and emotions are the children's bread and the Lord receives glory as we receive these love harvests from Him! I believe the harvest of answered prayer is upon us and all we have to do is to take hold of it. Do not neglect your day of visitation. Offer your prayer knowing prayers do change everything.

CHAPTER 11 - PRAYER CHANGES EVERYTHING

1. How can you circumvent a grass-is-greener-on-the-other-side mentality? Name a couple of times where you have personally grappled with this issue.

2. Name a couple of areas where our culture has superficially attempted to heal brokenness. For example, those who are calling on the legalization of all drugs treating the worst offenders as a medical condition is a superficial remedy.

3. Where have you been greedy and not just monetarily? How can you turn that greed into godly gain? For example, my greediness for position can be submitted to the Lord knowing I am positionally seated with Him in heavenly places, so I have everything I could ever want or need.

4. Include a meditation or devotion that has personally meant much to you. Read it over several times and ask what the Lord is saying to you!

5. Where has the Lord asked you to be a watchman on the wall?

6. When have you felt a check in your spirit? Name a time when you obeyed this kind of prompting and when you overturned it and needed to repent.

7. Where are there areas of provision you have despised because you did not recognize them as hidden manna?

CHAPTER 12 - HOW THE LEADING OF THE LORD WORKS

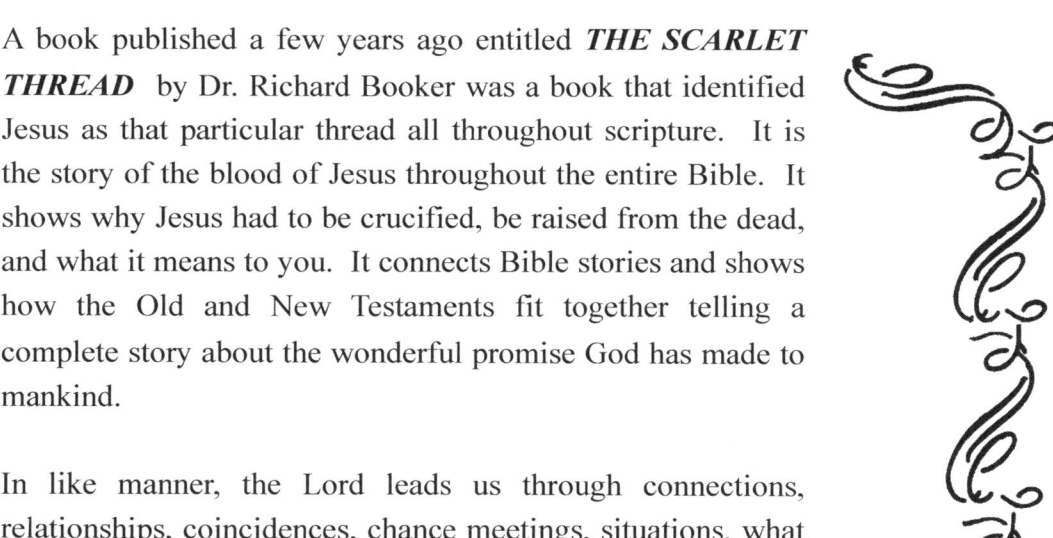

A book published a few years ago entitled ***THE SCARLET THREAD*** by Dr. Richard Booker was a book that identified Jesus as that particular thread all throughout scripture. It is the story of the blood of Jesus throughout the entire Bible. It shows why Jesus had to be crucified, be raised from the dead, and what it means to you. It connects Bible stories and shows how the Old and New Testaments fit together telling a complete story about the wonderful promise God has made to mankind.

In like manner, the Lord leads us through connections, relationships, coincidences, chance meetings, situations, what we may hear on radio or television. As what we encounter bears witness with our spirit or brings peace and joy to us, I think it is safe to say, we can proceed through that effectual door of opportunity. We can get bogged down when we confront a situation that seems blocked, inflexible, and intractable or has the potential of bringing strife into life. Such blockages need to be handled with tender loving care. We need to guard our reactions to these perceptions. Perchance the Lord will open one of these closed doors depending on how well we pass our test. The scripture of Psalm 27:14 comes to mind which says, "Wait on the Lord; be of good courage, and He shall strengthen thine heart; wait, I say, on the Lord." Patience is indeed a virtue.

We could surely avoid much devastation and calamity in our thinking and our lives if we did wait on the Lord and hear His wise and insightful instruction for us. It behooves us to discover and follow through on enacting our spiritual gifts, know some of our weaknesses and strengths, and develop the talents the Lord has loaned to us for a short while to fully utilize. Following the leading of the Holy

Spirit, entails an action and not just merely musing or daydreaming what one would like to see happen in one's life.

I have also found it includes networking and celebrating the victories and joys of others, not simply our own. In fact, the emphasis should be on others as indicated by Philippians 2:4 which tells us "not to look to your own interests, but each of you to the interests of others." When this habit can be cultivated with regularity, great peace and joy can be found as we are doing God's work, involved in the cry of His heart and trusting that He is indeed taking care of our personal needs.

It is important that we know the goal of following the leading of the Holy Spirit. It cannot be about promoting our own agenda or seeking a platform. Yet in the Lord's gracious timing, He may indeed provide opportunities to proclaim His interaction in our lives. Our responsibility is to stay in sweet communication with the Lover of our souls so we may know Him and His ways of love, service, candor, faithfulness and fruitfulness. Aren't these laudable goals for the type of resume and repertoire the Lord is building within us?

We become so enamored with the ways and thoughts of the Lord; there is room for nothing else. Then we are quick to follow the impressions, inclination and temperament of the Holy Spirit and do what He indicates. This is the narrow way He is leading us into – a way of protection, provision, mercy, courage and all that we could ever hope for or anticipate.

Like the Israelites, we sometimes want to look back to Egypt, but the times we are living in behooves us to see that is simply not an option. Neither do we want to become like Lot's wife and upon looking back become paralyzed and unable to move forward. That is the enemy's scheme and tactic with us.

We overcome that spirit of intimidation and take authority

in the power of the Holy Spirit to quench all the fiery darts of the evil one. This is what walking by the leading of the Holy Spirit allows. He gives us the confidence and gentle persuasion that His ways will remain, never to be uprooted and is everything we need. Isn't it worth submitting your entire life to His awe-inspiring, miraculous leading today?

CHAPTER 12 -HOW THE LEADING OF THE LORD WORKS

1. Have you ever equated Jesus, ***THE SCARLET THREAD***, being the story of His blood throughout the entire Bible? How do you feel about this discovery? How has the blood of Jesus impacted you?

2. How can you be of good courage when you do "commit your way to the Lord and know He will give you the desires of your heart"? In other words, how do you wait with grace, self-control, and enthusiasm for something you greatly desire?

3. What are some victories and joys of others that you can celebrate? List a few as an act of obedience to Philippians 2:4 mentioned in the article.

4. How has the Lord protected, provided, and shown mercy to you?

5. What are some fiery darts in your life and how can you take authority against them in the power of the Word and taking an action?

6. What are some ways the Lord has led you? You can include impressions, through His Word, attitudes, etc and be specific about what He is showing you.

CHAPTER 13 - BE THE LIGHT WHERE YOU ARE

I think we have sometimes misunderstood this admonition our Lord has given us in Matthew 5:14-16. In this passage, Jesus calls us to be the light of the world and a city set on a hill cannot be hidden. Later in the passage, Jesus tells us to let our light shine before others, that they may see your good deeds and glorify your Father in heaven. What's there to misunderstand you may ask? A lot, I will calmly, but not hopelessly, retort.

The world at large and the body of Christ in particular think this means having a substantial platform from which to impart beneficial advice or do deeds worthy of wide scale publicity. We as Christians believe we have a life-changing spectacular message that all the world should hear. We desire to embark on projects and programs that will have far-reaching impacts. However, before we go any further, I think it behooves us to look at two very faith-arresting verses. In the following New Translation Bible verse, it pleads in Matthew 6:4, "Give your gifts in private, and your Father, who sees everything, will reward you." In Matthew 6:7, also in the New Translation it shares, "But when you give to someone in need, don't let your left hand know what your right hand is doing."

These two verses have a lot to do with our faulty perceptions of what it means to be a light. It may in most cases, be that the only ones who see the expressions of love in word and deed is our Heavenly Father, His Son Jesus, and the Holy Spirit. To have an audience with these Divine Three, should be all that is necessary for us to know we have been received; however, as human beings we have insatiable appetites for more and are not easily satisfied. We desire the applause of our fellow man sadly, rather than the praise and commendation of the Lord.

It can actually paralyze us in moving forward in the things of God and the impact He wants to make through our lives. We need to ask ourselves what is the motivation for letting our lights shine before men. That can be a hard perception for us to reconcile with. It is so important to find our contentment in God alone, and let Him open up the opportunities He wants us to partake of. The problem is we think that opportunity is beneath us, doesn't show off our best side, or even short circuits what we think we can do creatively, spiritually and intellectually. When our recalcitrance is seen in that light (pardon the pun), our true motivations are exposed and hopefully bring us to the place of repentance that simply means a turnaround. In this case, it means turning towards God and His plans for our lives.

Have you noticed the Lord is intent on bringing down our high and lofty thoughts of ourselves? Is it because the Lord is petty, petulant, obstinate, over-bearing and all that we associate with ourselves or does He really know better? Speaking on the light, is it possible that being wrapped up in ourselves prevents us from seeing God Himself Who is the light of the world according to John 8:12? This verse goes on to say, "Whoever follows me will never walk in darkness, but will have the light of life."

No? Then what does it mean to be a light, a reflection of Jesus in our lives? I am learning the sheer joy of finding Jesus in all the nooks and crannies of life. According to Phyllis Shirer in her study of Gideon in the book of Judges, she remarks, "If we are constantly anticipating a grandiose event to accompany the times when we encounter Him or hear His voice, we will miss out on many intimate moments in our relationship with God. The mundane, the routine, and the commonplace – these are often the contexts in which He will reveal Himself to humanity. More often than not, flashy and flamboyant are not his style." I believe these sentiments blend well in what I am trying to convey.

Perhaps some of the greatest surprises in heaven will be open rewards regarding nondescript actions we took to be light to another and follow with corresponding actions. When I volunteer as a greeter or an altar counselor at a large women's conference, can arrange for others to go free, invite people to the numerous outreaches and ministries I am a part of, sending out texts, emails and Facebook messages of encouragement, notifying of something of interest or importance to my listeners, offering hospitality through meals I have prepared for an event, being willing to speak or listen at a moment's notice for the purpose of being a witness to Him, willing to be flexible and stretched in new ways that cause me to humble myself and lower my pride, this is what causes me to be a light in the world. The repetition, consistency, perseverance and, if you will, the practice of doing good, assuredly paves the way for the Lord to be able to entrust me with bigger and brighter opportunities which He Himself has ordained. I certainly don't want to miss those days of visitation, do you?

I trust we practice being His light in all the hidden areas in life He has made accessible and manifest to everyone who seeks, as we are told in scripture, they will find. This also reflects our Lord's character. He is infinitely humble, gracious, long-suffering, kind, and majestic. He wants to be found, but in the format He has ordained for us. To be a light, we must become like He is. James 4:10 is such a great verse to cling to as it tells us to "humble ourselves before the Lord, and in due time He will exalt or lift us up." This can be such a challenging principle as we often feel our due time has come and gone. This is the test of trust in the Lord's unfailing love for us. We honestly don't know what is best for us, but He always does.

Given this background and foundation, perhaps the Lord is bringing us to a place where He can entrust us with larger responsibilities and public exposure. He doesn't want us to crash and burn! There are few who can handle the spotlight platforms can afford. If they are self-made, forget it! In that case, the person herself needs to maintain the momentum, opportunities for ministry, speaking or contacts. With the Lord, He is the connector and He will sustain what He has originated. We need to live in the atmosphere of Romans 12:1 which says: "Therefore, I urge you brothers and sisters, in view of God's mercy, to offer your bodies as a living sacrifice, holy and pleasing to God – this is your true and proper worship. Do not conform to the pattern of this world, but be transformed by the renewing of your mind. Then you will be able to test and approve what God's will is – this good, pleasing, and perfect will." It requires sacrifice to be a light for the Lord and we are misled if we think otherwise.

We are to seek the Lord and His righteousness, and all these things will be added. The pearl of great price is the Lord. He is our reward, goal, objective and all who we aspire to be. As we become more and more acquainted with this reality and truth, we become more contented and acquire great gain. This is why we reflect the Light of the world. He is Who the world needs, not us.

As John the Baptist said in John 3:30, "He must increase, but I must decrease. " When we grab hold of this lifestyle, we will start to understand the Lord's directives in our lives. Be surprised and enthralled as He leads and where He leads you to go! He knows the way since He is the Light and will shine in your areas of darkness. Don't we want His Light illuminating our way said about us?

Follow the Light and not only brighten the corner where you are, but your family, church, community, city, state, country, then world. What a formidable task, but it starts with being obedient to shine in the crevices and nondescript places in your life. Why not shine for Him today?

CHAPTER 13 - BE THE LIGHT WHERE YOU ARE

1. How has the Lord used situations, people, circumstances and the Word to humble you?

2. Where have you walked in darkness willfully or unintentionally and how has the Lord shone His light upon your path?

3. What gives you great delight in doing what you don't even think about because the thrill of involvement is sufficient? This could be what you are rewarded for in heaven that you may just take for granted. Isn't that exciting to ponder on?

4. Can you recount times when the Lord has promoted you? Has it come after a time of humbling? Please share.

5. What are some greater responsibilities you would like to undertake for God's glory?

CHAPTER 14 - INTERRUPTIONS? ARE THEY ACTUALLY THE FATHER'S PURSUIT OF US?

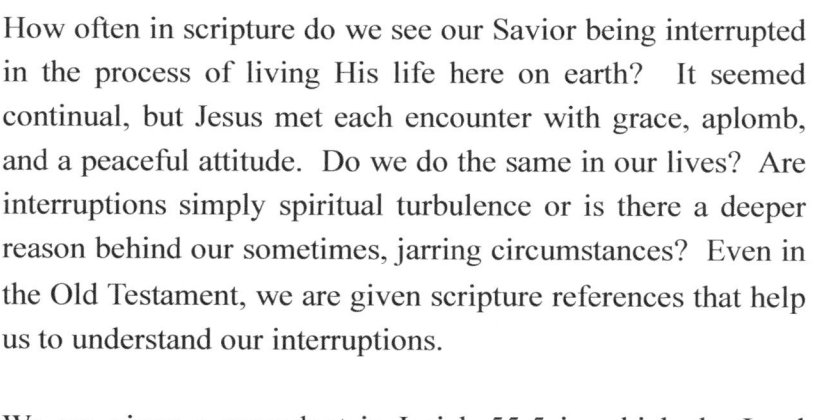

How often in scripture do we see our Savior being interrupted in the process of living His life here on earth? It seemed continual, but Jesus met each encounter with grace, aplomb, and a peaceful attitude. Do we do the same in our lives? Are interruptions simply spiritual turbulence or is there a deeper reason behind our sometimes, jarring circumstances? Even in the Old Testament, we are given scripture references that help us to understand our interruptions.

We are given a precedent in Isaiah 55:5 in which the Lord shows us His perspective on such matters. It says here: "My thoughts are completely different from yours," and "Your ways are far beyond anything you could imagine." Could this help explain the role these interruptions have?

Psalm 118:24 is a familiar verse, "This is the day the Lord has made. Let us rejoice and be glad in it." How many would think that as the Lord has prepared a day for us, this would also include interruptions in which have been fashioned and tailor-made for us God's purposes? It helps us to look at these inconveniences in a different light, and even put a positive spin on the whole matter.

Each one of the disciples were interrupted in their particular schedules whether it be as a fisherman, a tax collector, a Zealot, and most prominent of all, Saul when he was persecuting Christians on the way to Damascus. Jesus appeared to him, knocked him off his horse and caused him to be blind for three days so he would be in a more vulnerable position in order for Ananias to minister to Saul. Then he even had a name change to Paul. In all of these divine moments, Jesus said to these chosen ones, "Come, follow me." Do you suppose He asks us to do the same when He encounters us in disguise, unexpectedly, and asks us if we trust Him in these instances?

There were seemingly adverse circumstances for Paul when he was on the way to preach the Gospel. He repeatedly met with persecution and imprisonment. It was in prison where Paul wrote two thirds of the New Testament. What about the youngest disciple, John? After his enemy's attempt to boil him in oil failed, John was banished to the Isle of Patmos. That looked like a huge inconvenience! In fact, John had a heavenly vision and wrote the whole book of Revelation. Interruptions can take us to amazing pinnacles and heights that can benefit many, many others!

There are several definitions of interruptions. Some of them are the following: an act of disobedience, a break, disruptions, some abrupt occurrence that interferes in an ongoing activity, a pause, an intermission, a time interval in which there is a temporary cessation of something.

God-ordained interruptions are pregnant with meaning and purpose! How often do we need readjustments in our lives? We would be right to say every day. Wouldn't it be better even to say every moment? Joyce Meyer is asked how she keeps her priorities in balance with the abundance of responsibility she has. She says the key for her is she is consistently straightening out her priorities. I am sure it is accompanied with a lot of interruptions. We can't just coast along when we are interrupted. We are confronted with making choices or decisions that will impact our lives and others.

We are given an opportunity to respond with negative fruit resulting in a bad attitude or respond with humility and a display of good fruit that we have been developing if we look to the Lord. We then are teachable, easily led by the

Spirit to walk in His good plan for us, can credibly instruct others and give off a pleasant sweet smelling fragrance (Ephesians 5:2) or perfume to others, to inspire, exhort and lift up others. All of this is a by-product of interruptions.

When we are interrupted, we may feel tempted to become disgruntled because our plans were disrupted or tampered with. As we are honest with ourselves, it is because of our pride and our desires for self-elevation that were affected.

Truly being healed is living before an audience of One in Three Persons, God, the Father, the Son and the Holy Spirit. He is the one who really matters since out of that understanding, we are able to treat others in the best possible manner.

CHAPTER 14 - INTERRUPTIONS? ARE THEY ACTUALLY THE FATHER'S PURSUIT OF US?

1. What do you consider spiritual turbulence in your life and could these be considered interruptions? Name some and how the Lord has used these for good purposes.

2. Name two other biblical examples of godly interruptions in which Jesus worked miraculous signs.

3. Can you name a plan or two you had and the Lord took you in a different direction? How has this resulted for you and can you see God's Hand working on your behalf?

4. What is your understanding of being a "co-heir with Christ" (Romans 8:17) and how have you entered into this lifestyle with Jesus?

CHAPTER 15 - MOVE FORWARD FOR GOD'S WILL IN YOUR LIFE

How often do we find ourselves in this, from a natural standpoint, precarious position in life? Remember the man by the Pool of Bethesda who lay there by the pool for 38 years! That was a long time and he obviously lived with excuses in his life for not moving forward. Not until Jesus came, and asked if he wanted to be made whole or well, was this man confronted with his travesty which is a representation of something in a false and distorted way. Why would I say this? According to Jesus, this man had the opportunity of being well when the man lived with hopelessness and much pity and disdain for his condition. Jesus made it clear to this man this perceived inability to become well no longer needed to plague him.

Do we not have our own Pools of Bethesda? Isn't the issue just as prolonged in our lives and with the knowledge of Jesus as our Savior, are we not met with the Pool every day? We can choose to enter into the healing waters of the Word, walk in the Spirit, and act consistently in agreement with our Lord's prescription for health and wholeness. It is important to set our minds regarding this posture of faith. There is no greater adventure in living than to do so!

Why do we then get stuck? Sometimes we are looking back to something in our past about which we want to restore or use to prop up our flagging identities that should be strongly rooted and grounded in God's love (Ephesians 3:17). Unfortunately, in our society and more so really than any time in history, we are in competition with one another's idols, instead of being inspired with one another's love and actions for the Lord. Matthew 5:16 attests to this when we hear, "In the same way, let your light shine before others, that they may see your good deeds and glorify your Father in heaven" and in 1 Peter 2:12 which encourages, "Live such good lives among the pagans that, though they accuse you of doing wrong, they may see your good deeds and glorify God on the day he visits us." When we are busy as believers following the admonitions of these two preceding verses, what time do we have in looking around us to see what others are doing, having, saying, unless it is in alignment with God's Word. Otherwise, we are simply to love others, believer or non-believer and let the Lord speak to their spirits.

Sometimes we are desirous of doing something so magnificent we can glory in it, rather than in the Lord. I think this is one of the reasons He tells us not to despise the day of small things or small beginnings as Zechariah 4:10 shares, for the Lord rejoices to see the work begin. I think He also rejoices for us to stay small in our own eyes, in order for God to be large in us and for us to be able to hear His voice when He calls.

Sometimes we don't move forward because anything innovative from the Lord challenges, undoes us, intimidates us. We get used to how life has been lived heretofore and after all, a person who we may admire attained their success by staying with the tried and true methods. I believe as far as scripture is concerned we never leave the basics, the rudimentary elements of our walk with the Lord, but as Hebrews 6:1-3, we are to move on to maturity. These are uncharted waters since becoming mature in the Lord necessitates we have a close relationship with Him and this requires a fresh, vibrant walk with Him everyday. We can stay in our safe ruts and refuse to move on with Him and He certainly will still love us, but we will remain babes in Christ and most likely carnal in our interactions with others and within ourselves.

Just as only eating dessert would be very unsatisfactory after a while and would deprive us of very necessary nutrients for strength, alertness, and health, we cannot afford as believers to only be able to drink milk and not eat the meat of the Word. Hebrews 5:12 refers to us this truth. This truth, then, begs the question what does it mean to eat the solid food of the Word. Here are some scriptures that refer to this very important process for the Christian's growth. Some in the Old Testament are: Deuteronomy 8:3, "Man does not live by bread alone, but by everything that proceeds through the mouth of Jehovah", Job 23:12, "I have treasured the words of His mouth more than my apportioned food," Psalm 119:103, "How sweet are your words to my taste! Sweeter than honey to my mouth," Jeremiah 15:16, "Your words were found and I ate them and Your Word became to me the gladness and joy of my heart…" In the New Testament, we can find in I Timothy 4:6, "being nourished with the words of the faith and of the good teaching which you have closely followed," and in Revelation 10:8-10, "…take it and devour it…and I took the little scroll out of the hand of the Angel and devoured it, and it was as sweet as honey in my mouth, and when I had eaten it, my stomach became bitter."

Each one of these verses are treasures and food for our spiritual appetites and welfare! How do we then see the application of this spiritual action be made manifest? This is where the proverbial rubber meets the road, no doubt. How can Christians resist the tendency of gravitating towards spiritual milk and move towards the eating of spiritual meat? One obstacle is a reluctance to or a sluggishness regarding the digging into deeper truths. There is laziness and apathy towards spiritual development.

There is also an inability to articulate one's faith or sharing anything new that a person has discovered about Christ. This can also be a way the enemy has a hook in us, so we can be drawn back into the world and its ways. Ephesians 4:22 admonishes us to put on ways of living that reveal our new natures in Christ. There is also an inability to self-feed or to discern between good and evil. Thank God for His Holy Spirit Who lovingly convicts, guides us back into truth and will teach us the error of our ways and lead us higher into the green pastures which Psalm 23 so wonderfully expounds for us.

Are we indeed teachable? Ah, there's the rub! As we stir the gifts that are within us, show the love of God by helping His people, be diligent to the end, and do not become weary in well doing, we will be demonstrating the maturity necessary in order to move forward in the Lord's will for us.

It seems more and more as we do grow in the Lord, His will is not only a destination, although we do know heaven is our home, but it is a state of mind, living in the Presence of the Lord, communing with Him and the journey of being changed from glory to glory (2 Corinthians 3:18). He will most likely lead into areas in which He can display the gifts He has given us, but He also likes to demonstrate His strength through our weakness as 2 Corinthians 12:9 indicates. It behooves us to know when He is leading us to move forward on a gifting, talent, or skill He has given us, if we are to learn something new, or simply rest in His loving care.

To move in the flow of the Holy Spirit is the most glorious transition a child of God can possibly desire this side of heaven! As we do this, we can be assured we are moving forward in the strength, wisdom, power, love and peace of God! In closing, I share the familiar and extremely effective verses: "Trust in the Lord with all your heart and lean not on your own understanding, In all your ways, acknowledge Him and He will make straight your paths" (Proverbs 3:5,6). I do believe we can safely move forward as we pray, study His Word and become a doer of the Word. In so doing, He is removing the obstacles, those sins about which so easily entangle, and heal us body, mind and spirit. What an exciting prospect for each of us who truly want to grow in the power of His might and in His spirit, for this is His highest Will for us to discover and abide in.

CHAPTER 15 -MOVE FORWARD FOR GOD'S WILL IN YOUR LIFE

1. What excuses or denials are you making for not moving forward in your life What is one of your Pools of Bethesda?

2. Describe the adventure of having a posture of faith in your life. Give an example when you needed to stand in faith for something you perceived as difficult. Share the result.

3. What are a couple of small beginnings in your life that you have seen the Lord enlarge and bring about great fruitfulness in your life?

4. What is a rut in your life that you believe the Lord is calling you to lay aside and enter into a fuller relationship with Him? What does that look like practically speaking?

5. Name something on your Bucket List that you could equate with a spiritual desire. What steps can you take towards its emergence in your life?

CHAPTER 16 - WHAT DOES IT MEAN TO BE COMPLETE IN CHRIST?

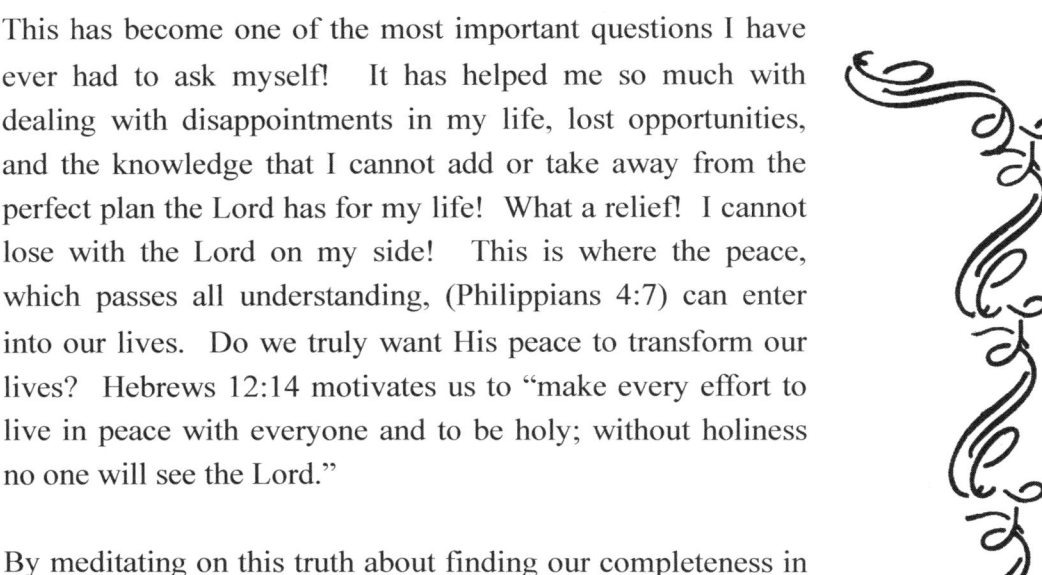

This has become one of the most important questions I have ever had to ask myself! It has helped me so much with dealing with disappointments in my life, lost opportunities, and the knowledge that I cannot add or take away from the perfect plan the Lord has for my life! What a relief! I cannot lose with the Lord on my side! This is where the peace, which passes all understanding, (Philippians 4:7) can enter into our lives. Do we truly want His peace to transform our lives? Hebrews 12:14 motivates us to "make every effort to live in peace with everyone and to be holy; without holiness no one will see the Lord."

By meditating on this truth about finding our completeness in Christ, the tendency we have to compare ourselves with one another or thinking whatever we do doesn't really cut the mustard, can be erased. Anxiety can be removed, since often we have excess stress because of unreasonable expectations about others and ourselves.

Insecurity can be removed since when we know we are totally fulfilled in Christ's love for us. We can move away from the longing of constant validation from others because the Holy Spirit is constantly reinforcing us. Others cannot possibly give what only the Holy Spirit can give and He is so able to do beyond what we can ask or hope for. We can then give others the freedom of being who the Lord uniquely has made them and don't have to long to be like them, but be who God has made us to be.

When we are filled with this wonderful knowledge of the Lord being are all in all, it changes our perspective completely. One of the major advantages, I believe, is avoiding the tendency we all have to berate or reproach ourselves for areas we have judged ourselves unworthy, imperfect, for lost opportunities and so forth. The ancient pagan groups were known for cutting themselves and bloodletting in order to appease their idols. That may sound a bit stark and unnecessary to bring up with this topic, but this is precisely the point.

We don't have the same kind of idols these heathen groups had, although there is a resurgence of paganism plaguing our world today. We do harbor other idols that can be tangible, but often they are subtler and are inner idols. The Message Bible in Ezekiel 14:1-5 indicates this truth so well. Here goes! "Some of the leaders of Israel approached me and sat down with me. God's Message came to me: 'Son of Man, these people have installed idols in their hearts. They have embraced the wickedness that will ruin them. Why should I even bother with their prayers? Therefore tell them, The Message of God, the Master: All in Israel who install idols in their hearts and embrace the wickedness that will ruin them and still have the gall to come to a prophet, be on notice: I, God, will step in and personally answer them as they come dragging along their mob of idols. I am ready to go to work on the hearts of the house of Israel, all of whom have left me for their idols.'"

So we see in this passage the Old Testament does not merely mention outward idols, but also inner idols. In our modern culture, we are prone to think we only have inner idols, but if truth were known, we have our modern outer idols just as much as they did in the Old Testament. Idols can never satisfy, complete, fulfill, or give us purpose. We must be more cognizant of all our distractions and the sin that so easily entangles (Hebrews 12:1). In my own case, I can get caught up with all the marvelous events and opportunities to attend and at which to serve. Serving is a good thing, but not for the purpose of serving my idols. It is important to be mindful of what is truly beckoning.

As we find our sense of completeness more and more in Christ, Who loves us perfectly and enables us to navigate through the treacherous waters of life, our joy quotient can certainly surge. It is time we ask ourselves, is what we really want in life, to be more and more conformed into Christ's image? He is our Alpha and Omega, our First and Last and holds the key to true living. In a recent Joyce Meyer program, I witnessed a good visual pertaining to being complete in Christ and wholeness. She referred to Romans 8:29 which clarifies "For those whom He foreknew He also predestined to be conformed to the image of His Son." She showed us a pretty slab of clay, pink in color, probably for all the women in attendance, and this represents us, the clay. A cookie cutter gingerbread man represented Jesus. The clay needed to be pressed into the cookie cutter shape. One of the problems, though, is all the excess outside of the image of Christ. This clay needed to be discarded in order for the image of Christ, or for our purposes the gingerbread man, to be revealed. It can then be seen we reflect His image perfectly when there is nothing of us hanging on.

As we discard and let go of our notions of what we want to be and allow the perfect image of Jesus to radiate in our lives, we can come to that completeness in Him in which He so wants for us and can truly satisfy our souls.

CHAPTER 16 – WHAT DOES IT MEAN TO BE COMPLETE IN CHRIST?

1. Give some examples of peace that passes understanding. What brings you peace?

2. What are two insecurities you have and how are you taking action to overcome these insecurities?

3. Can you think of some other visual examples like the clay and the cookie cutter which would give you a concrete view of how we become predestined into the image of Christ?

CHAPTER 17 - CONTENTMENT IS NOT JUST A "NEW YORK STATE OF MIND"

The "New York State of Mind" song by Billy Joel was never a hit song, but became a fan favorite and one in which was played regularly at concerts. Its inspiration was undoubtedly the love and enthusiasm Billy Joel had for New York after returning there from living in Los Angeles for a few years. The song was honored also in a concert for the families of first responders after 9/11 and played again for Sandy Relief at Madison Square Garden in New York City. The melody has a soothing quality and it is not surprising that saxophonists hailed it for conveying such sounds on their instruments, having soloed this song for studio versions. (https://en.m.wikipedia.org/wiki/new_york_state_of_mind)

On a topic of contentment, one wants to find inspiration, comfort and above all, a peaceful state of mind. Contentment can have the elusive quality of a butterfly. Sometimes it doesn't take much distraction to brush contentment off or away. Because of strongholds, un-forgiveness, pride, lack of depth for finding satisfactory solutions for our lives, we stay cemented in a state of mind in which is fraught with anxiety, depression, and a profound lack of peace.

This is not the state of mind Paul is mentioning to Timothy in I Timothy 6:6 when he communicates godliness with contentment is great gain.

From an article entitled, "Why is Godliness with Contentment Great Gain?" the author Pastor Colin S Smith mentions quite a few good truths about this subject. To highlight a few, Pastor Smith says, "Bring your desires down to the level of your possessions." "The rare jewel is not found when you have more, but when you have less." " Learn to enjoy what God has given more than you grieve over what He has taken away." "Practice the art of godly contentment and you will find that it is great gain."

What wise words and insights. I would add too it is not playing catch up by envying a measure of success some one else has, but learning from it. We can be content because we live in God's loving Presence and He values us for exactly who He made us to be. There doesn't need to be that ominous foreboding feeling of dread and dismay because we have not lived up to our expectations, since they are faulty anyway. We can have goals and aspirations without making them golden calf idols. For the believer, there is an innate sense of peace that communicates to us we are already complete in Him. There is a growing sense of trust that God supplies all of our needs according to His riches in Glory through Christ Jesus.

Riches are fleeting, temporary and cannot be taken with us into eternity. Our true riches are the ones that have been chiseled in furnaces of affliction through much ruminating and meditating, bouts of self reproach, discouragement and then draw into the will of God as we have made right decisions.

Just like distractions can cause the butterfly effect in our lives to change the trajectory of our life's path, contentment as a butterfly can stay with us as long as it is not disturbed from its perch. What exactly is the butterfly effect? It is the sensitive dependence on initial conditions in which a small change at one place in a deterministic nonlinear system can result in large differences in a later state. The theoretical example given is a hurricane's formation can be contingent on whether or not a distant butterfly had flapped its wings several weeks earlier. (n.m.wikipedia.com/butterflyeffect)

Contentment cannot be boxed in captivity. It has to be free to breathe and alight on a receptive soul. Otherwise, contentment dies away and is not able to flow in the trajectory of the Holy Spirit. This is not something we can merely grasp by our intellect. It is as the saying goes caught not taught although in practicing contentment in our lives we are indeed taught by it!

How is contentment cultivated? Many things which have seemed so important in our quest for meaning and tranquility die when we confront the acquisition of peace and a sense of well being. If we attempt to hold on to inconsequential substances either tangible or intangible, we will be sorely disappointed and grieved to despair! Certainly, these need to be dealt with sternly and resolutely, so we do not oppose ourselves in the process of finding contentment.

Recognizing God's Presence is truthfully the pearl of great price that we are commissioned to seek for with our whole heart, soul, and mind. When we value contentment as that premier jewel, we will not hastily cast it off, no matter if providing a harbor for it, makes sense to our minds or not. As if on cue, interestingly enough, the parable of the pearl of great price appears in only one of the Gospels, in Matthew 13:45-46. In it, the pearl illustrates the great value of the Kingdom of Heaven whose chief characteristic I might add is the attitude and state of bliss or contentment. In some writings on this topic, the pearl is pursued with much diligent seeking. Also, those who do not believe in the kingdom of heaven enough to stake their whole future on it are unworthy of the kingdom. I think it behooves us then to find contentment and not be shocked as we enter eternity because we did not cultivate that attitude innately as we lived here on earth. As we do this, we will be put on display someday before the host of heaven as we have been fitted just like a pearl had been formed in the innermost recesses of an oyster.

Having authentic godly contentment is better than a New York state of mind. It is a divinely peaceful state of mind which does not have to be fleeting, but one in which we can abide in as John 15:4 indicates. How marvelous is that not only in concept but also in actuality! A refrain from a song in a particular season called "This is my Grown Up Christmas List" says:

"No more lives torn apart
That wars would never start
And time would heal all hearts
And everyone would have a friend
And right would always win
And love would never end."

(Composed by David Foster, and lyrics by Linda Thompson-Jenner, sung by Amy Grant)
This is another good definition of what true contentment is! Are you encouraged to cultivate and maintain contentment in your life today? Rest in that knowledge. Resist the temptation to take matters in your own hands. Trust the Lord to give you that divine state of mind today!

CHAPTER 17 – CONTENTMENT IS NOT JUST A "NEW YORK STATE OF MIND"

1. Can you give an example or two of why godliness with contentment is great gain?

2. Name two verses on contentment. How are you going to be more proactive in guarding your heart to receive more contentment in your life?

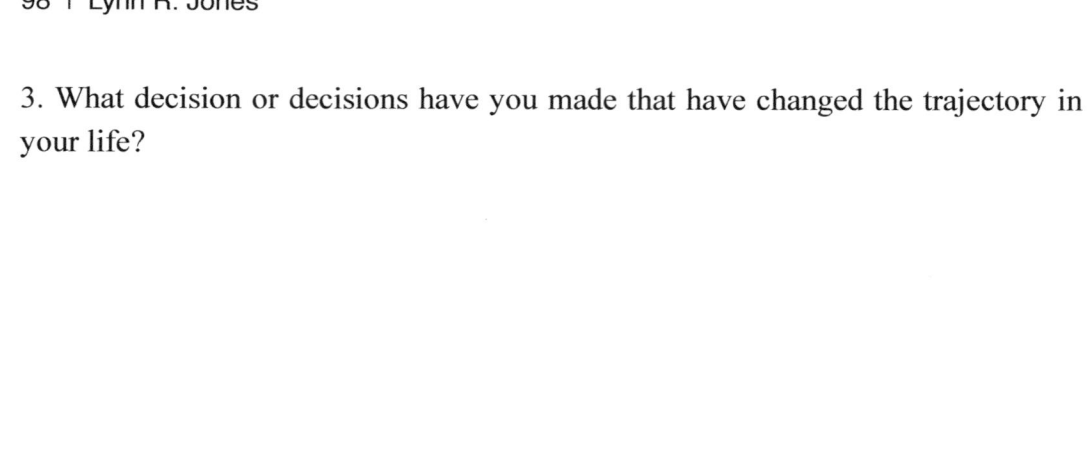

3. What decision or decisions have you made that have changed the trajectory in your life?

4. Would you include the lyrics of a song that for you reflects contentment in your life or what you perceive is more contentment that you would like to acquire?

CHAPTER 18 - WHAT ARE SOME OF YOUR "FAVORITE THINGS?"

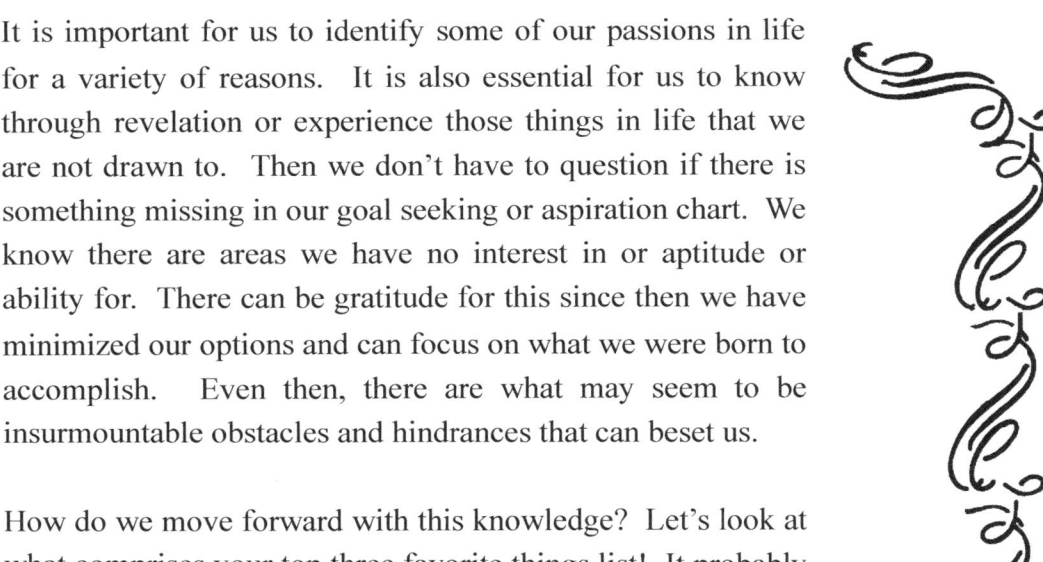

It is important for us to identify some of our passions in life for a variety of reasons. It is also essential for us to know through revelation or experience those things in life that we are not drawn to. Then we don't have to question if there is something missing in our goal seeking or aspiration chart. We know there are areas we have no interest in or aptitude or ability for. There can be gratitude for this since then we have minimized our options and can focus on what we were born to accomplish. Even then, there are what may seem to be insurmountable obstacles and hindrances that can beset us.

How do we move forward with this knowledge? Let's look at what comprises your top three favorite things list! It probably has changed somewhat as you have grown older. I know mine has. For example, I started out in college as a music major. I loved music and played piano and sang. I wanted to go into contemporary Christian music, but then along the way, I discovered a former opera diva who taught voice in the college town I resided in. I had always enjoyed light opera, languages, wearing fancy clothes and the beautiful sets this genre of a musical career offered. The former opera star accepted me as one of her students and I would travel to her lovely home for lessons. I had my way mapped out if this was the pattern I wanted to follow. However, a couple of things happened along the way. I found out I was rotten in music theory, but more importantly, I saw some things about opera which curtailed my progress in this direction. At that time in my life, there were not too many Christian opera singers that I had heard of. My scope of influence seemed very narrow indeed.

The librettos or stories I would be singing in song were usually not very edifying and more like a soap opera. To be really good at this profession, most everything else in my life would have to take a back seat or cease to exist for me. In short, I felt the Lord was saying to me, He would be at the doorway waiting for me to come back and follow the path He had for me. Now, even though I dropped my music major and changed to English, I have always enjoyed music and have used my talents for accompanying or singing in choirs or solos as the opportunity arose, but it seemed clear the Lord was tailoring this interest of mine down to the size He wanted it to take in my life.

Since that time, I have had the honor and privilege of teaching in a private school capacity, homeschooled all four of my children, and taught at various homeschool co-ops in various capacities such as teaching history, English literature, writing, speech, geography, and beginning Spanish. It was a thrill to help my children or others know how to write better, catch a concept, or be able to speak better when delivering a speech. I learned so much whether it was through research for good materials to use or helping a remedial level student go to a higher place academically and measure that progress in grade form. It was a season that formed me as a person and helped students transfer in some cases from homeschool to public or private education and be able to take advanced placement classes in English or writing primarily. It also was a sense of accomplishment towards which continued to spur me on to where I presently find myself engaged. It was indeed a season of life for which I am thankful, but not a stopping place for me.

As the Lord has chiseled and fine-tuned me, I have come into areas in life that I can say have become my top three candidates for the Lord's plan for me. Yes, I enjoy sewing the occasional needlepoint, taking a good hearty walk, visiting with friends, volunteering at Christian conferences in various capacities, cooking a good meal, and travel, but these are peripheral to the core of the Lord's call for me.

Because of my work in prayer counseling in the past and

present, I started to see I might have an aptitude for pastoral care. This was followed up later with opportunities to help those in my family struggling with emotional issues that stymied their growth, career opportunities and relationship with God and others. I endeavored to take various counseling classes that were fashioned to address deep inner healing issues that could take the form of understanding the role of forgiveness, bitter-root judgments, inner vows, expectations, and many other healing subjects. It has been revolutionary in so many ways and has led me to thinking more about ministry, whether it be through counseling, doing chaplain work, and prayer ministry where the Lord's signs and wonders are seen in more and more dramatic ways.

Because of the Lord's drawing into these areas, I have placed before Him the need for Bible school or advanced training through possibly a Master's degree in counseling. I am excited about these prospects and know the Lord can open doors when there seems to be no open door. In identifying this passion to help others in the areas of deep emotional wounding, I have seen through my studies how I have been helped and want to pass this understanding to others for their own breakthroughs. When there is an accompanying joy or excitement that characterizes our pursuits, we can know we are on the right track for further clarification to be made available to us.

The second and third areas of concentration for me have been in developing my writing and speaking gifts rather than my singing that I now relegate to praise and worship or in soaking prayer atmospheres. I have had the opportunity to share my testimony and aspects of a book I have authored entitled ***CONFESSIONS OF A BLONDE***. I am presently engaged in a focus on my writing. You are now reading my second book ***SOAKING MOMENTS WITH LYNN***. I have also had the opportunity to do a newsletter for one of the churches I attended in the past. There are opportunities to sell the books and I trust more speaking opportunities will follow close on those heels.

Proverbs 18:16 joyfully proclaims, “A man’s gifts will make room for him, and brings him before great men.” It certainly seems important to understand what our gifts are so the Lord can indeed make room for the utilization of them.

Apply diligence to those gifts and watch the favor of the Lord take over! Then we can stand back in awe knowing He was the one who opened those doors for us which seemed effortless as if we had nothing to do with it. The Lord takes our little mustard seed of faith, our efforts, and multiplies it into something glorious beyond our expectations.

As we allow ourselves to be the palette, our Master Artist can apply His brush strokes upon our life and create the masterpiece we always believed resided in us. As we believe, we do receive. It is a faith walk we take one step at a time. Remember, God’s gifts and calling are irrevocable, never change, and are without repentance. We can just say the word to our loving Father, who can bring a wilted gift and call it back to life. Step into service and watch resurrection principles take place. Employ what God has given you to accomplish.

CHAPTER 18 – WHAT ARE SOME OF YOUR "FAVORITE THINGS?"

1. Just for fun, name three career choices you would have no interest in personally and so can cross this off your list of potential career opportunities.

2. Now brainstorm and write down on one or two pages all the things you would like to do, ministries you are interested in, career opportunities about which might be of interest, hobbies you want to explore. Don't spend too much time thinking, and give yourself 5-10 minutes to do this exercise.

3. Narrow this list to your top three interests and then circle one. Name these three and why you circled the top interest.

4. It is never too late to pursue your dreams and visions. What would it take for you to acquire the skills and tools you might need to follow through on this dream? Why not do it?

CHAPTER 19 - BE OPEN TO CHANGE

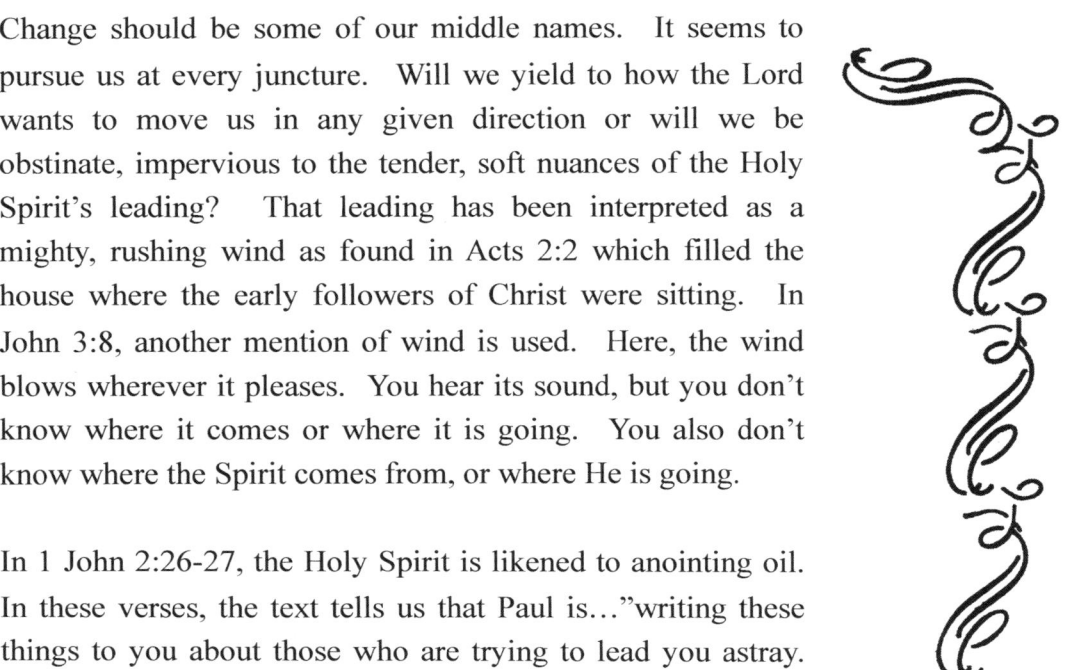

Change should be some of our middle names. It seems to pursue us at every juncture. Will we yield to how the Lord wants to move us in any given direction or will we be obstinate, impervious to the tender, soft nuances of the Holy Spirit's leading? That leading has been interpreted as a mighty, rushing wind as found in Acts 2:2 which filled the house where the early followers of Christ were sitting. In John 3:8, another mention of wind is used. Here, the wind blows wherever it pleases. You hear its sound, but you don't know where it comes or where it is going. You also don't know where the Spirit comes from, or where He is going.

In 1 John 2:26-27, the Holy Spirit is likened to anointing oil. In these verses, the text tells us that Paul is…"writing these things to you about those who are trying to lead you astray. As for you, the anointing you received from Him remains in you, and you do not need anyone to teach you. But as His anointing teaches you about all things and as that anointing is real, not counterfeit just as it has taught you, remain in Him."

The parable in Matthew 25:1-13 informs us of the ten virgins waiting for the bridegroom, five of which had no oil in their lamps which is akin to having the Holy Spirit. The Holy Spirit is likened to a dove who hovered over Jesus at His baptism in Luke 3:21. He works quietly often behind the scenes determined with our permission to work His life-producing results of peace, love and joy into our lives. Isaiah 44:3 likens the Holy Spirit to water. This verse says: "For I will pour water on the thirsty, land and streams on the dry ground; I will pour out my Spirit on your offspring, and my blessing on your descendants."

Another famous passage is from John 7:37-39. In it, Jesus says, "If anyone thirsts, let him come to me and drink. Whoever believes in me, as the scripture says, Out of his heart will flow rivers of living water. Now this He said about the Spirit whom those who believed in Him were to receive…" These are just a smattering of thoughts and ideas based on the Holy Spirit Who is the agent of change in our lives.

Why do we often resist change in our lives? It means we are usually entering into unknown territory. We must learn to trust with regularity the One Who says, "I am the Way, the Truth and the Life. No one comes to the Father, but through me." (John 14:6). Jesus came to show us the Father and in the Prodigal Son story, Luke 15:11-32, the Father receives His son with open arms, with joy and without condemnation. When we understand the Father's heart revealed in His Son, change for our good, will be welcomed and embraced.

The greatest adventure in life is following hard after the Holy Spirit. Recently, I think, I am more closely understanding what it means for a man to plan his ways, but the Lord orders and directs his steps. What I am discovering is every time I have my own expectations or plan my own way, I am greatly disappointed, embarrassed, and even ashamed. Why? Because nothing compares with being in God's Presence and knowing consistently He has the best path for me to follow. I am tired and disgusted with bad fruit in my life. Recognizing by trusting God's will for me as James 4:15 informs us, "If the Lord wills, we will live and do this or that," I am in a much better frame of mind.

As ironic as this may seem, the type of change the Holy Spirit works in a person's life actually brings a restful attitude. I am experiencing this phenomenon more and more in my life. Truly, we have everything we need and the tools to accomplish God's will in our lives when we do look to God's Word to be our necessary soul food and drink. There is a wonderful hymn that has recently come back to my remembrance. The chorus starts with the title. It goes like this – "Love lifted me, Love lifted me, When nothing else would do, Love lifted me." It is so true when it is God's Love, honored and revered above all else.

God's changes in our lives are always for our good. So again, why the resistance? I have mentioned the flesh, but there is also an enemy of our souls, the devil himself, and his minions! Ephesians 6:2 tells us, "For we do not wrestle against flesh and blood, but against the rulers, against the authorities, against the cosmic powers over this present darkness." God always has a better idea! Romans 8:17 instructs us as children, co-heirs of Christ, if indeed we share in his suffering in order that we also may share in His Glory." Interruptions can be a form of suffering which the Lord can so easily turn around for us to see we can be a part of His divine plan of redemption and restoration. It ultimately results in commendation, giving new meaning to Jesus' admonition to come and follow Him (Matthew 11:28). Can we trust Him with our interruptions? Since He has ordained them, I believe so!

CHAPTER 19 – BE OPEN TO CHANGE

1.Can you tell the difference between being anointed or having the grace to share God's truth with others or when it is your own opinion? How can you tell? Give an example or two.

2. What does it mean to thirst or hunger after the Lord in your life? Where do you have the most enthusiasm (meaning inspired by God) in your life even if it is sometimes challenging? What changes are you willing to make?

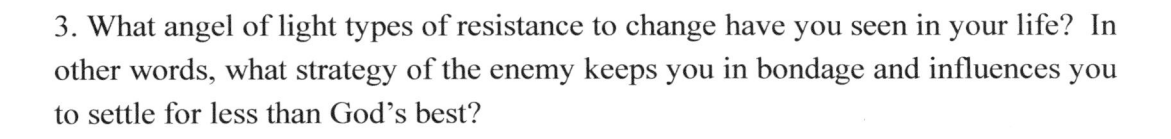

3. What angel of light types of resistance to change have you seen in your life? In other words, what strategy of the enemy keeps you in bondage and influences you to settle for less than God's best?

4. Enumerate a couple of areas the Lord has enabled you to trade your ashes for His beauty.

CHAPTER 20 - RECOVERING FROM PERFORMANCE ORIENTATION

What is P.O. as it is called in its abbreviated form? The short answer is doing anything from a wounded heart. Many types of public figures such as pastors, singers, actors, and speakers do precisely this. They even might do quite well in their field, but inside they are a pack of un-forgiveness, bitter root judgments, and have a very low opinion of their own self worth. The difference between the one who is healed and the one wounded is motivation. The incentive for the wounded one is to gain people's approval or earn favor even from God. Neither are helpful places to be. The healed person is motivated by the knowledge that he or she is loved by God and is complete in Him. Therefore, all activity is accomplished from the overflow and knowledge of scripture found in Philippians 2:13 which joyfully asserts, "It is God Who works in you both to will and to do of His good pleasure." What a comforting, free, blissful, and restful thought! I don't have to stress, compare, cajole, coerce, be pushy and certainly don't need to be tyrannical in the worst-case scenarios.

This can be a tricky character flaw to work through! Sometimes in the process of healing, a person who is used to being a doer, an activity planner, a punctual scheduler or the many other activities a doer is compelled towards, goes to the other extreme and is tempted to (or drops) everything. There is balance which is needed while in the process of discerning what is needed in life.

In this celebrity culture that we live in, we are used to hearing the term diva thrown about recklessly to describe a new singer, actress or lady of renown. It has been recently that I have coined the phrase about being a recovering diva because I believe my sights were on some career that would cause me to shine and for people to take note of. Now, this sounds perfectly plausible in the days we are living in, but through often painful inventory, I have come to see this should not be my purpose. Instead, I see it is the Lord who I want to magnify! He is the One Who has given me everything I could ask or hope for -my life, talents, gifts, significant people who are His appointed networkers for me, opportunities, attainable goals with His help. There is nothing I can add or take away from the love He lavishly bestows on me. I am ostensibly complete in Him.

When our props, our idols, our works are taken away, rather than feeling depleted, we should see all were burdens, entanglements, the sin which so easily besets us, as Hebrews 12:1 mentions, fall under the category of either performance orientation or actual rebellion to what the Lord's plan is for us. When we look at P.O. from this dimension, it definitely sheds a helpful light on the subject. It shows the absence of the Lord's blessing too which is something we do not want to entertain.

There is this human tendency to help God out with His plan for our life and performance orientation is only too accommodating to lend that helping hand. The problem is that often we can see nothing wrong with this modus operandi because it appears we are accomplishing something of merit and acclaim. We applaud these traits disproportionately to what our motivation really is. First Samuel 16:7 testifies man looks on the outside, but the Lord looks upon the heart. We have our values turned inside out and as a result we suffer from defeat, rejection, frustration, and all the works of the flesh. It is a vicious cycle which only the Lord can break by His Spirit and impartation of His truth in our lives.

Since we are so heavily bombarded by our society by idols and corruptible things, it will warrant our focus, devotion, and astuteness to those areas that matter to God. We will need to rightly divide the Word and check our motivations on a daily basis.

How do we move forward then in the Lord? The old tried and true ways may actually be a deception since it is highlighting how we can exalt ourselves and not the Lord. I think the verse from Zechariah 4:10 says it so aptly in the New Living Translation. It says to not despise the days of small beginnings, for the Lord rejoices to see the work begin. Don't we often do just this and don't want to wait for God's perfect timing in our lives? In doing so, we often employ the tactics of performance orientation and even get by with our innate talents and gifts for a season, but unless the foundation is on the Rock, it will be a sinking sand type of enterprise.

How do we not succumb to this strategy? We must honor God, His Word, and His Spirit in our lives. If we are yielding to all Three, then there is no room for the flesh to glory and we can have peace within. Peace, I think, needs to be valued more than it is and we need to pursue it as a pearl of great price to the exclusion of all lesser gods which are really imposters. Let us yield our faulty understandings of success and progress up to the Lord and know when we are following Him, our path is sure, steady and secure.

Let's get our focus oriented onto the Lord and what He has already accomplished rather than our performance and get ready to embark on adventures of a lifetime each and every day. Joshua 1:8 tells us, "This Book of the Law shall not depart from your mouth, but you shall meditate in it day and night, that you may observe to do according to al that is written in it. For then you will make your way prosperous, and then you have good success." This is how we move forward and trust the Lord to open and shut doors for us. Living in this heaven sent atmosphere is far better than what we can concoct on our own. Let's lay our performance orientation ways at the foot of the altar never to be picked up again. I am praying for your success in Him, dear reader. You are already a success in Jesus! Bravo!

CHAPTER 20 -RECOVERING FROM PERFORMANCE ORIENTATION

1. Do you see performance orientation as an addiction in your life? How so and what is one recovery strategy the Lord has given you to implement?

2. Can you name instances where you stress, compare, cajole, coerce, are pushy or tyrannical?

3. Is there another type of addiction in your life you are recovering from? Can you share it and what is your strategy for overcoming?

4. Have you ever given God a helping hand as Sarah attempted to do when she gave Hagar to her husband Abraham as a wife (found in Genesis 16:1-4) in order to follow through on God's promise of giving Abraham a son?

5. What are small beginnings in your life and how has the Lord blessed you in the midst of your perception of smallness?

6. Brainstorm some examples of peace in your life and be astonished how it will lift your spirit!

CHAPTER 21 - EMBARKING ON A NEW CAREER OR MINISTRY?

Sometimes it takes a lifetime to find one's calling in life. Many times, I think it is an amalgamation of pieces to a cosmic puzzle. It may be that there are so many areas of interest that we pursue and indulge in because of the various gifts, talents and aptitudes the Lord gives each one of us. It is often hard to focus on just one thing, but when we look over our lives we see a strong recurring theme. What motivates our passion?

Where do we see recurring success, fruitfulness, recognition because of the Lord's work in our lives? This is where we will experience the greatest joy and peace. It seems to have a direct effect with the concept of abiding in the vine found in John 15. What a delightful concept for us to grasp as we embrace it and not deviate from it. In this chapter in scripture, we are told, God the Father is the gardener and He prunes us for greater fruitfulness.

Perhaps this is why it seems at times to take so long for us to find our purpose in life. Could it be we are being pruned for our greater purpose for the Lord's Glory? Moses is one of our greatest examples of pruning that we see in scripture. We are introduced to Moses as a baby who is being salvaged from the Pharaoh's injunction to kill all the Hebrew boy babies because the Hebrews were multiplying too fast. Pharaoh's daughter rescued Moses by drawing him out of the waters. This action gave him the meaning of his name. He then was raised amongst great luxury, privilege and reputation. Many historical scholars believe Moses was groomed to be the next Pharaoh. Then Moses discovers his true identity. He is not Egyptian, but Hebrew.

Aren't we like this sometimes? We have labored under a pseudo identity thinking we should be fulfilled in a certain lifestyle or way or style of thinking, because the outer conditions seem to line up contributing to our perfect concept of what is acceptable in our lives. Because of an encounter we may have with the Lord, we discover more of what should be in our lives and what should not. Consequently, we have a choice to make.

Moses decided to take matters into his own hands once he was awakened to his true identity. He saw the oppression of his own Hebrew people and killed an Egyptian with his own hands who was beating a Hebrew slave. Because of this action, he jeopardized his own standing not only with the Egyptians, but with his own people who brought this matter to Moses' attention when Moses stepped in to prevent a conflict between two of his countrymen fighting. They saw Moses' hypocrisy and indeed, Moses was banished by the Pharaoh because of his actions.

Do we risk stalling the Lord's plan in our lives because we have acted prematurely by taking matters into our own hands? It is not the end of the world, but we may have been able to make greater progress for the Lord's glory if we had not made a pre-emptive strike. How wonderful it is for us to know and ponder the ramifications of Romans 8:28 which tells us the Lord works all things for our good according to all who have been called according to His purpose. The Lord can "restore to you the years the locusts have eaten (Joel 2:25)."

We know this is true because of what happened with Moses. Yes, he spent 40 years in the backside of the desert while God was honing his shepherding skills to lead people eventually while he labored as one who tended actual sheep. Ironically, the Egyptians detested shepherds and considered them the lowliest of all careers and Moses had been a prince of Egypt.

After those 40 years of pruning and testing, Moses had an encounter with the Lord that he would never forget. He met

God through the burning bush. This account is chronicled for us in Exodus 3. Perhaps it is when we go through our times of cleansing of our presuppositions, our orientations, our misplaced opinions and biases, we can have our own burning bush experiences with God when we start to recognize His Presence in our lives like no other time before. If Moses needed this experience to prepare him for his role of deliverer of 2.5-3.5 million Hebrew children, can we escape pruning for the tasks the Lord has for us in preparation for the new roles the Lord has for us to play? I don't think so.

A person in history whom Roman Catholics venerate as a saint is Francis of Assisi. I mention Francis because like Moses he was raised in abundance and in luxury. His call to a new identity and burning bush experience occurred as a young man probably a little younger than Moses who was banished at the age of 40. While he was enjoying worldly pleasures and dressed in the best of silks as his father was a merchant and his mother, a noblewoman, Francis experienced a reality check. He saw the condition of so many others around him living in abject poverty and gave one beggar all that he had. Afterwards, he decided to join the ranks of the poor and became for all intents and purposes their patron saint. He endured the anger of his father for making such a decision, but there is no doubt Francis raised the level of the social consciousness of his time by choosing to go a different route than what his family and what he expected to pursue.

Other distinctions both men, Moses and Francis, share is they had great periods of solitude, perhaps more so in Francis' case as he lived as a single man. Francis was actually described as the "Apostle of Silence." During the Middle Ages in which historians refer to as the Dark Ages, Francis was seen as one of the few bright lights of that time. Thomas of Celano, a Franciscan Friar and poet said of Francis, "He was always occupied with Jesus; Jesus he bore in his heart, Jesus in his mouth, Jesus in his ears, Jesus in his hands, Jesus in the rest of his members." This is indicative of Francis being foremost a worshiper. The art of worshiping God in silence was summed up in a famous statement referring to Francis. It said, "Go everywhere and preach the gospel to everyone. And if you absolutely must, use words." Francis may have been a man of few words, but he was a man of great power, very likely because of his times of solitude. (en.wikipedia.org/wiki/Francis_of_Assisi)

We know from scripture that Moses, being a shepherd, spent countless hours with sheep. He learned to be quiet in his spirit amongst the bleating of sheep. Perhaps Moses became acquainted with quiet for so long, this is why when the Lord asked him to speak to Pharaoh about letting the Hebrew people go and then leading those same people out of Egypt, he said to the Lord, I cannot speak. Perhaps this time of solitude also enabled Moses to hear the Lord most acutely when He conveyed His warnings to Pharaoh about what he would do in response to the Pharaoh's frequent refusals to grant Moses Yahweh's desire!

Because of his single mindedness, Francis took the remarkable stance of traveling to Egypt and preaches to the Sultan during the times of the Crusades. How like Moses was he in his calling to preach to the potentate of that time. Francis felt led to do so and even endure martyrdom if it was called for. Would Francis have had the same impact if he had stayed the son of a wealthy silk merchant and enjoyed the prosperity that this type of life warranted? Would another deliverer have eclipsed Moses' life, if Moses had chosen an easier way to live out his life? We cannot know, but the plight of the poor and a great respect for creation has been accentuated because of the life of Francis who some have called Saint. The formation of the Hebrews was forged as a mighty nation in which the Lord would continue to do His miraculous interventions.

What passion is calling you to make a difference in your world and for God's glory? Are you willing for your world to be rocked? Losing ourselves in the areas the Lord has uniquely gifted us for is a gift I believe we don't want to miss receiving. Can the Lord tailor make for us His yoke He tells us to take upon us in order to facilitate our lives and bring fulfillment beyond our fondest dreams? Through the pruning process and the removal of chaff in our lives, we can have a much clearer view of what is truly important to us and what our identity in the Lord is meant to be.

Is the Lord calling you out, drawing you out from many waters (2 Samuel 22:17) in order to accomplish His perfect plan for your life? Can we give Him permission to reshape our lives to give us the maximum opportunities to make a difference in this world? There is never a too late perspective we should have, but instead an expectation the Lord is working in us both to will and to work for His good pleasure (Philippians 2:13).

I have mentioned two historical figures who were given great privilege and honor in their earlier years, who had an abundance of the world's pleasure and either by default in Moses' case or personal choice, in Francis's case, lived a simpler and more modest life in their most publicized years. The Bible has something to say about this that can help us understand why they lived their kind of lives. James 4:4 admonishes us friendship with the world makes you an enemy with God. Do you need to give up all your worldly goods in order to find God's best? Not necessarily, but do find out what the Lord wants you to do with any wealth He gives you the power to create.

What an exciting discovery lies ahead of you. The Lord will show you the way, and He will never let you go.

CHAPTER 21 - EMBARKING ON A NEW CAREER OR MINISTRY?

1. What pseudo identity have you labored under like Moses? Where have you seen fruitfulness in your life? How is this helping you see your true identity in Christ? Give scripture verses.

2. Can you identify other historical figures in history who made drastic changes as Moses and Francis did for the glory of God? How can this serve as an inspiration to you and what changes is the Lord asking for you to make?

3. Spend some time, about 30 minutes at least, in meditative silence and soaking music. Write down what you hear the Lord speaking to you.

CHAPTER 22 – DEALING WITH THE STUBBORN STAINS IN OUR LIVES

What is a stubborn stain? All of us can probably think of a spot, a blemish, an unsightly speck on a favorite garment we own, or on a piece of furniture, or on a car we treasure. It is a nuisance, a bother, in some cases, a great grief (if we have to throw the garment or piece of furniture out, usually not the car), or an embarrassment. If it is not too big of a stain, we usually learn to live with it. If it is a bigger stain, we will suffer some kind of loss whether it is financial, emotional or relational. The word stain makes me think of a tiny or large grotesque teardrop that immediately connotes to us the feeling of sadness. I think this is how the Lord looks at the stains in our lives. Ephesians 5:27 (AMP) presents to us: "that He might present the church to Himself in glorious splendor, without spot or wrinkle or any such things" (that she might be holy and faultless). In the Message Bible, the same scripture communicates endearingly, Christ's love makes the church whole. His words evoke her beauty. Everything He does and says is designed to bring the best out of her, dressing her in dazzling white silk, radiant with holiness. WOW! I really like how the Message Bible puts it. When we know how much we are loved by our Bridegroom, Jesus Christ, it definitely causes us to be drawn closer to Him and desire to do the things that will enable us to be the best we can possibly be!

What makes us think we can handle our small stains or even that we will simply tolerate them? I believe at the root of such thinking is we esteem ourselves more highly than we ought. There are several scriptures this subject addresses. Let's look at some of them. Roman 12:3 (AMP) tell us, "For by grace (unmerited favor of God) given to me, I warn everyone among you not to estimate and think of himself more highly than he ought (not to have an exaggerated opinion of his own faith apportioned by God to him)."

Ecclesiastes 7:16 offers: "Be not (morbidly exacting and externally) righteous overmuch, neither strive to make yourself pretentiously appear) over-wise – why should you (get puffed up) and destroy yourself (with presumptuous self-sufficiency)?"

First Corinthians 13:4,5 (AMP) exhorts: "Love endures long and is patient and kind; love is never envious nor boils over with jealousy, is not boastful or vainglorious, does not display itself haughtily. It is not conceited (arrogant and inflated with pride); it is not rude (unmannerly) and does not act unbecomingly. Love (God's love in us) does not insist on its own rights or its own way, for it is not self-seeking; it is not touchy or fretful or resentful; it takes no account of the evil done to it (it pays no attention to a suffered wrong).

There is also Philippians 2:3,4 (AMP) cautioning us this way. "Do nothing from factional motives (through contentiousness, strife, selfishness, or for unworthy ends) or prompted by conceit and empty arrogance. Instead, in the true spirit of humility (lowliness of mind) let each regard the others as better than and superior to himself (thinking more highly of one another than you do of yourselves). Let each of you esteem and look upon and be concerned for not (merely) his own interests, but also each for the interests of others."

This is by no means an exhaustive list of scriptures on humility, but it is at least a start. When we realize what foolish pride can do to us according to God's Word, it is worth paying attention to the little specks in our character that could grow into the huge log we are admonished to take out of our eye before we attempt to correct another. We find this principle in Matthew 7:5. It comes down to awareness about what God's Word tells us are defects in our character and actions. Are we willing to yield control to the Lord rather than believe we can hide from Him as Adam and Eve did in the garden?

It is indicative when we persist in a line of erroneous thinking, we have missed the mark in this area. It is up to us if we want to suppress what we know to be true, be in denial and then justify a particular type of behavior. It is important as Song of Solomon 2:15b instructs: "It is the little foxes that spoil the vines." In modern vernacular, we should be so observant in our lives, when it comes to bad deportment, language or thought patterns that we nip it in the bud at the onset.

When it comes to the church and particularly, the bride of Christ today, if we are not careful, we can become enamored with the honored role the Lord has bestowed on us by virtue of His grace. By so doing, we start seeing ourselves above the main and adjust to our sin, rather than come to the Lord and confess our sins to Him.

1 John 2:1 (AMP) presents this remedy. John writes to us affectionately, "My dear children, I write you these things so that you may not violate God's law and sin. But if anyone should sin, we have an Advocate (One Who will intercede for us) with the Father – (it is) Jesus Christ (the all) righteous (upright, just), Who conforms to the Father's will in every purpose, thought and action."

Those stains we tolerate are simply sins which we are admonished to relinquish control of to Jesus Who will intercede for us so we are not seen as violators, criminals, or not adhering to the requirements for intimate fellowship with God.

Another reason we hold on to those stubborn stains small or large, is because we begin to identify with those sins and have a distinct, distorted, false sense of belonging. The temporary satisfaction sin brings, the counterfeit sense of adrenaline or thrill we can embrace, or the deception we can fall prey to since

according to 2 Corinthians 11:4b, satan himself masquerades as an angel of light, are all great temptations to lure us from our true identity in Jesus Christ. Disregarding the Lord's still, small voice of conviction over a period of time can reinforce the deception until yielding to the temptation actually becomes a stronghold (2 Corinthians 10:4), which the Bible tells us is to overcome and demolish. We can even think after a while our stains look good on us; it doesn't matter what people think (or God for that matter), and we are free to parade in our stains for the whole world to see.

If the pretense goes this far, I think you have an idea of what a stronghold can actually do to an individual, then a group of people, a community, and have far-reaching implications for our cities, states, our country, and the world. It is clearly necessary to clean house and trust the Lord to do the work in our lives that only He can do.

In fact, Isaiah 64:6a (AMP) shares, "For we have all become like one who is unclean (ceremoniously, like a leper), and all our righteousness (our best deeds of rightness and justice) is like filthy rags or a polluted garment..."

Why would we want to be clothed in such a manner when we are conversely told in Isaiah 61:3 (KVJ), "...to give unto them beauty for ashes, the oil of joy for mourning, the garment of praise for the spirit of heaviness, that they may be called trees of righteousness, the planting of the Lord that he might be glorified."

The Lord would say to all of you who do mourn in Zion, He does not want you to be downcast any longer because of the burden of hiding your stains small or big. No more rationalizations excuses, or deceptions. His Arms are open and His Hands are large enough to enfold all of the stains, blemishes, and filth you want to give Him. He would also proclaim that you underestimate His Ability, His Love, and His Desire to follow through with His Promises to you.

You are so easily distracted by the enemy's flashy show of false brilliance, when I, says the Lord, want to give you a consistent flame of fire that can be seen beautifully, clearly, and abundantly. It will shine upon you and overtake you, so that you reflect Me so magnificently, that the enemy must flee since he recognizes your association, relationship, and intimate friendship with Me. So let Me adorn you with My Beauty, My Radiance, and My Glory. Did I not write to you that you could be constantly transfigured into My image in ever-increasing splendor and from one degree of glory to another? Why would you want to settle for anything less when I have so much to offer you? My gifts are unending, breathtaking, spectacular, overflowing, and unsearchable. I want you My child to savor all that I have for you and to be clothed as my very Own. You are part of my Bride and I desire to showcase you as a sign and wonder to the world. I will use the splendor I have imparted to you to bring all men to my Son, Jesus. Do not delay! Lay every spot, burden, impediment, and obstacle down at the foot of the cross and let Me amaze you with the Great Exchange I am making as a result of your actions.

The antidote for stubborn stains in our lives is to apply the Lord's Healing Presence and allow Him to clothe us with the garment of salvation, cover us with the robe of righteousness, as a bridegroom decks himself with a garland, and as a bride adorns herself with her jewels (Isaiah 61:10). We can then more fully embrace with great vigor the plans and most importantly, the tender and depth-defying love our Lord has for us. Let's embrace this love together.

CHAPTER 22 - DEALING WITH THE STUBBORN STAINS IN OUR LIVES

1. What would you consider a stubborn stain in your life? Name a couple and write down two scriptures other than what has been given in the article which would address this problematic aspect of your life.

2. What would you constitute a log in your eye versus a speck in your brother or sister's eye? Name an example of a particular situation in your life that would illustrate this principle.

3. Name an area about which you have been in denial and how have you tried to justify it. Did it work for you? What steps if you haven't already taken to rectify it?

4. Where do you have distorted, false senses of belonging or identity? Why in spite of knowing holding on to the counterfeit could hurt your testimony and more importantly hurt the Lord, is it difficult to let go of these falsehoods?

5. How can you more fully and successfully meditate on the beauty of the Lord? What would this look like? Be creative. Perhaps drawing a picture, composing a song, working on needlepoint or embroidery, walking outdoors in nature, take a train ride and journal about your trip or something else that could spark your passion for the Lord. Reading scripture and listening to praise music is always good. If you listen to the Word as well as praise music, you could add a creative flair to your meditation.

CHAPTER 23 - OVERCOMING FEARS

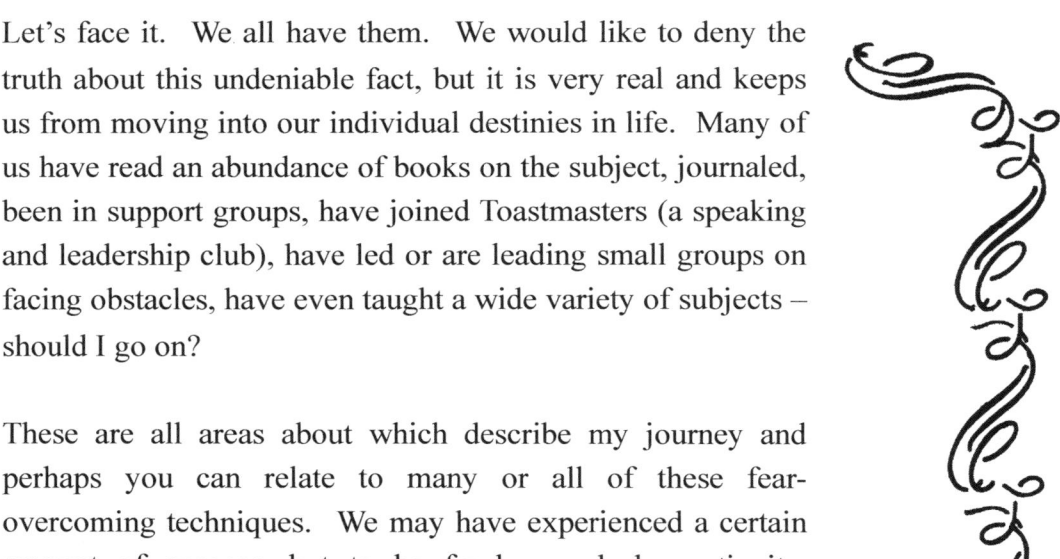

Let's face it. We all have them. We would like to deny the truth about this undeniable fact, but it is very real and keeps us from moving into our individual destinies in life. Many of us have read an abundance of books on the subject, journaled, been in support groups, have joined Toastmasters (a speaking and leadership club), have led or are leading small groups on facing obstacles, have even taught a wide variety of subjects – should I go on?

These are all areas about which describe my journey and perhaps you can relate to many or all of these fear-overcoming techniques. We may have experienced a certain amount of success, but to be frank, we lack continuity, momentum, or the confidence we are accomplishing great things in life. We endeavor to multi-task in an effort to discover something that will ignite and take off like a shooting comet in our lives, but so very often they sizzle at the launching pad, die down to a simmer or go up in smoke. We commence our tasks in a spirited fashion, but get so easily sidetracked and perhaps it is just easier to retreat into backgrounds that don't require much of us and where we can simply hibernate.

Second Timothy 1:7 shares, "For God did not give us a spirit of timidity (of cowardice, of craven and cringing and fawning fear), but (He has given us a spirit) of power and of love and of calm and well-balanced mind and discipline and self-control' (AMP). Is cowardice what we really want? Deep in our hearts, I don't think so.

Some of you are in dead-end jobs, relationships, even ministries and there is a tremendous need for some revitalization. Because you have tried so many avenues, the tendency truly is to think the unique dream we have had for our lives will not or cannot come to pass. Why succumb to this temptation?

The result, so familiar to many of us is a dull throbbing of the desire to be in another dimension or atmosphere. Our realization is we have indeed deferred the most vital tasks for another nondescript time. It occurs to me this pattern is not unlike anyone who is attempting to break a non-productive habit or addiction. It is because it is familiar and even though we could advance, prosper, be fulfilled through much needed change, we don't and stay in our stubborn well-worn ways. What will give us the kick in the pants to make the crucial difference in our own lives?

By way of example, I can share that a few years ago, I was visiting Six Flags over Texas with family and friends. It had been seven years since I had visited and I had made it clear I was very content seeing the shows, going on the water rides (in 100 degree heat, the water would be most refreshing), and the non-challenging rides. This time, my middle son reminds me in just a few short years, my ability to ride some of the more strenuous roller coaster rides might be greatly limited. Perhaps it was his enthusiasm for me to ride the notorious Titan ride, the late hour of the day, or the fact that I had just disembarked from the Superman ride and now felt I had supernatural stamina that I had agreed to ride the Titan. He talked me through this ride, told me to exhale before we made the 200 foot drop, so I wouldn't black out as others had mentioned they had felt, and voila – I made it through and lived to speak about it.

Well, this was a fear I assuredly overcame that day. This is only one example of an overcoming experience I think needs to be one of many in my life from now on.

This is how continuity can flow without interruption.

This is how momentum is created for positive change.

Then confidence is free to soar as wings as eagles.

I am reminded of a truth according to Isaiah 40:3, “Those who wait on the Lord (who expect, look for, and hope in Him) shall change and renew their strength and power; they shall lift their wings and mount up (close to God as eagles mount up to the sun); they will run and not grow weary, they will walk and not be faint or become tired.” (AMP)

Let us put traction to these faith filled words and move forward not just in word, but also in deed. My supposition is – we will never want to live in paralyzing fear again. We will be so inspired and emboldened to inscribe a new pattern in our lives in which non-productivity and fruitlessness is erased in us for a very long time.

Here’s a question to think about. What is a new pattern of thinking, talking and acting you can implement in your life today that can help you move forward and break out of the bondage of fear, immobility and frustration in your life?

CHAPTER 23 - OVERCOMING FEARS

1. Where are you multitasking currently? What is working and what is sizzling out or dying down to a simmer? What tools will you need to be more fruitful in the area which is gaining some traction or you are succeeding in?

2. Can you name a time in your life when you were given a kick in the pants? How did it change you?

3. Are you paralyzed in any area of your life and how can you confront it successfully?

4. Where are you lacking continuity, momentum, or confidence?

CHAPTER 24 - SAND CASTLES

Recently, I have had the occasion in prayer to hear a very interesting phrase as I was seeking the Lord for many concerns. These are common concerns that beset us regarding foundations for faith, wisdom, foolishness, perseverance, and even devastation. Before I share it, let's take a peek at these scriptures. In both Matthew 7:24-27 and Luke 6:47-49 (Message Bible), therein lies the parable of the two builders.

You know them; the one who built his house on the rock, the other built his house on the sand. The first version of the story from Matthew says this: "These words I speak to you are not incidental additions to your life, homeowner improvements to your standard of living. They are foundational words, words to build a life on. If you work these words into your life, you are like a smart carpenter who built his house on solid rock. Rain poured down, the river flooded, a tornado hit – but nothing moved that house. It was fixed to the rock. But, if you just use my words in Bible studies and don't work them into your life, you are like a stupid carpenter who built his house on the sandy beach. When a storm rolled in and the waves came up, it collapsed like a house of cards."

A second version of the story from Luke explains the parable in a different version. It goes like this: "Why are so you polite with me, always saying Yes, sir and That's right, sir, but never doing a thing I tell you. These words I speak to you are not mere additions to your life, homeowner improvements to your standard of living (repetition from the scriptures is good). They are foundational words, words to build a life on. If you work the words into your life, you are like a smart carpenter who dug deep and laid the foundation of his house on bedrock. When the river burst its banks and crashed against the house, nothing could shake it; it was built to last. But if you just use my words in Bible studies and don't work them into your life, you are like a dumb carpenter who built a house but skipped the foundation. When the swollen river came crashing in, it collapsed like a house of cards. It was a total loss."

There are similarities in both to emphasize the importance of this teaching. In Luke's version, an actual rebuke is given. It is not enough to go through the motions of congeniality and be a "Yes, man", but not following through to the task at hand. For our purposes, I want us to focus on Matthew 7:25 and Luke 8:48 and 49. In these verses, it says rain poured down, the river flooded, a tornado hit, but nothing moved that house. Luke says the house was built to last; nothing could shake it. It was built to last. In Matthew 7:26 and 27, the house is said to be built on the sandy beach and when the storm rolled in and the waves came up, it collapsed like a house of cards. Luke says the stupid carpenter skipped the foundation. When the swollen river came crashing in…it was a total loss. Back to Matthew 7:26, the house was built on the sandy beach. The sandy beach lacked substance, no cohesiveness, and therefore could not hold up against the stormy ocean waves.

Am I getting closer to the Lord's words to you regarding this teaching as a foundation? I hope so. Now, I want to take you to Imperial Beach, California. There is an Open Sandcastle competition every year in July. It is the championship of sand castle building where professional sand carvers vie for the title of Master Champion. There is more than $21,000 in cash prizes. Sandcastle building begins at 9:00 AM and concludes at 2 PM. Sculptures are only available for viewing until 4 PM due to the tides. These are beautiful masterpieces and are greatly admired by scores of people. Pictures are taken which will keep the image of that sand castle immortalized at least during our earthly lives. What is the big deal about sand castles? We all enjoy them and admire the immense talent it would take to construct such an edifice. A little lesson on sand sculpting may be helpful.

Good sand sculpture sand is a little like the world. It is somewhat dirty, having silt and clay that helps lock the irregular shaped sand grains together. The world has as a common fellowship, sin, which acts as a counterfeit bond, not of true agape love, but as a common problem. For the purposes of sand sculpture, the fine grains of sand can adhere to one another due to the right amount of water forming little bridges among the grains of sand and are analogous to the vulnerabilities we have as people unless we have something more substantial that can combine the grains altogether. Because of fine grain gaps, too much additional water fills the spaces among the grains, breaking down the bridges, thus lowering the surface tension, resulting in the sand flowing more easily, and causing the entire structure to collapse. The sharpest mixture of fine and coarse sand granules is most important to achieve good sand construction results. (en.wikipedia.org/wiki/Sand_art_and_play)

It is interesting to note that fine granules which have been rounded by the natural influences of seas and rivers (the world) negatively influence the bonding among individual granules as they more easily slide past each other. The sharper the sand, the better the bonding and unity taking place. It is not any different for the disciples of Christ who through discerning the thoughts and intentions of the heart (Hebrews 4:12) and walking circumspectly and not as fools (Ephesians 5:15), is sharpening his/her faith perspective and ability to walk in unity with fellow believers.

I can also apply sand castles to the passages in Romans 1:22a, professing to be wise, they became fools. Our own fabrications have become our gods. We are deceived into thinking the more we can devise and imagine apart from the Lord, we have entered into new revelation and enlightened understanding in which II Timothy 1:6 mentions is a doctrine of demons. This is becoming more apparent in the times we are living in. Because of prayers that seemingly have gone unanswered, disappointments, trials, and as many of us do believe, living in the last days as well, has ushered in more demonic activity.

However, it is a glorious time to be alive. The Lord is shining forth more brightly than ever before if we desire to seek Him with our whole heart, mind and soul (Deuteronomy 4:29). He is showing His children that the firm foundation of building our houses on the rock is what will stand, not the sinking sand, as opposed to sand castles, which can be built beautifully, creatively and quickly with no foundation.

Rock foundations need time for construction purposes. Someone has said stonework at its best is an incredible meditation. How much truer when we are building towards an eternal inheritance. (www.weblife.org/cob//cob_028.html)

There is an order when putting together a rock foundation. It takes time to see what shapes you need and which rocks fit where instead of using your own muscle to lift and fit them together through guesswork and supposition. Again, in the Christian life, when we take time to meditate on God's Word, and lean on His strength instead of our presumed know how, we will be able to receive the instructions and guidance He wants to give us. Proverbs 3:5,6 (AMP) bears this out so well by saying, "Lean on, trust in, and be confident in the Lord with all your heart and mind; and do not rely on your own insight or understanding. In all your ways know, recognize, and acknowledge Him, and He will direct and make straight and plain your paths."

In constructing a rock foundation with another person, it is important to be careful of one another's fingers and toes in particular that they might not be injured. How much more spiritually should we be, mindful of one another and exemplify considerate character as we interact together.

The biggest, heaviest stones should be placed first and accordingly, in a spiritual foundation, the most important and elementary principles need to be first emphasized and highlighted. Hebrews 6:1-2 elucidates these for us such as the foundation of repentance from dead works, faith toward God, doctrine of baptisms, laying on of hands, resurrection of the dead and eternal judgment. Going on to perfection as Hebrews 6:1 tells us this can only be done when these elementary principles are firm and secure much like what is needed in a rock foundation for the next layer of rocks to snuggle and rest on.

Cracks in a rock foundation need to be filled in stones into the right position whereby there is stability and a prevention of the stones coming apart through water or other pressures from outside forces. Spiritually, we may detect cracks in our lives by not being adequately armed with the full armor of God according to Ephesians 6:10-17. It is important that we rightly align ourselves with God's Word and our responsibility toward one another.

What a contrast we have between our beautiful sand castle type thinking and having our lives built on the rock foundation of God's Word. In a life worth living for the Lord, the emphasis in our lives is rightfully so, the foundational principles. After this is in place, then our path has been set and what we build on it, although important as we yield to the Lord's working in our lives, is secondary in importance to the foundation. In building sand castles in our mind, that is the only thing that is important since again there is not a sound foundation upon which to build.

It is also important to examine our lives as Acts 17:11 and 2 Corinthians 13:5 indicate and test ourselves as to whether we are in the faith or not. The understanding about how we build our lives can be a powerful indicator. As we are secure our spiritual house is built on the rock foundation, we can move fearlessly and freely into the realm of glory that II Corinthians 3:18 tells us we can aspire to.

This is our inheritance as sons and daughters of the Most High God. It is time to be discerning and know how to divide truth from error. I encourage you to rejoice with exceeding joy as we apprehend the truth about foundations in God's Word and not be caught in the trap of producing an overly intricate sandcastle such as those in the contest at Imperial Beach, California, but is dissolved in one huge tidal wave. Build your house on the rock of God's Word and open yourself to all that the Lord wants to pour out upon you. His ways are unsearchable and unfathomable. Let's together move beyond earthly constraints and soak into the heavenly air of the Lord's atmosphere. Instead of building sand castles, build a rock foundation and pursue rock climbing instead.

CHAPTER 24 – SAND CASTLES

1. What in your life has collapsed like a house of sand or you felt like a swollen river has come crashing in? Please give examples of both.

2. Can you name a counterfeit bond in your life? How did you discover it was a counterfeit and how did you take action to resolve it?

3. Please give an example of unity among fellow believers. Jesus prayed in John 17 we would have unity with one another. Please give a personal example and also in one regarding what you have observed in your church that would indicate Jesus' prayers are being answered.

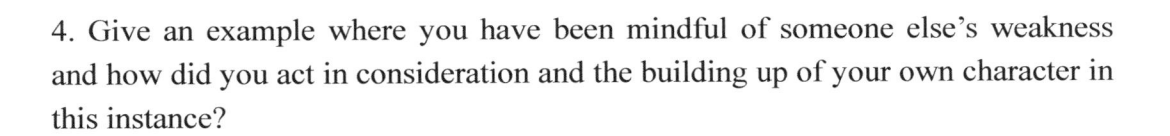

4. Give an example where you have been mindful of someone else's weakness and how did you act in consideration and the building up of your own character in this instance?

5. Where are there cracks or insecure places in your life needing stability? Use Acts 17:11 and 2 Corinthians 13:5 to help you with this exercise. How can you secure these areas?

6. What is your spiritual rock climbing pursuit? How can you use the tools in this article to help you with this pursuit?

CHAPTER 25 - THE LIFE COACHING CRAZE

Whatever happened to good old fashioned counseling? Is it still okay to get counseling or do we now need to go through the life-coaching route? It is important, I believe, to define our terms.

Valerie Burton, an actual life coach and author of books on these topics, superbly explains what life coaching is. One such book is called ***WHAT'S REALLY HOLDING YOU BACK***? It addresses many issues that are raised in life coaching settings such as helping clients determine and achieve their personal goals. As opposed to actual counseling, coaching is not targeted at psychological illness and coaches are not considered therapists and consultants. Among life coaching techniques, are mentoring, values assessment, behavior modification and behavior modeling.

"Counseling or psychotherapy is designed to improve the mental health of a client or patient, or to improve the mental health of a client or patient, or to improve group relationships as in a family. Among those who perform counseling, therapy is given in response to clinically diagnosable and/or existential crises. Various forms of therapies are offered to address the sensitive, deeply personal, and usually troubling topics that can assail individuals. Counseling can be long term and in depth often concerning one or two major issues whereas life coaching helps to equip you with the necessary tools to boost your growth, eliminate negativism and self-defeating habits, and set constructive goals relating to relationships, finances, spiritual life, career and health." (List of counseling topics from Wikipedia)

Counseling concentrates on going deep into a possible traumatic area that needs resolution whereas life coaching is broader in scope and going in depth is designed to propel you to breakthroughs in various areas of your life. It is important to understand the reason we are a certain way or repeat certain patterns of self-destruction. Counseling is also geared towards creating success, but greater attention may need to be given to the various wounds and emotional baggage a person may be carrying before they can even begin to have a vision of success in their lives. Both may be necessary in a person's life and one is not greater or better than the other. Through counseling, a problematic area can surface that perhaps needs more scrutiny and care than life coaching could help solve. Both disciplines work like a hand in a glove fashion. They are very similar, but their differences complement the other.

So what's the craze all about? As we are working through our problematic areas, we are rediscovering all the potential successes and victories we have stored up and we are re-energized to follow after our life's dreams and goals instead of settling for mediocrity and so much less than God's best for us.

We are learning not to short change ourselves or sabotage our efforts because there are so many helpful tools available to us for the accomplishing of our goals. Life coaching emphasizes being positive and how essential it is to have the right attitude, heart and words in order to arrive at your desired destination. It is a tool to help people who want to get unstuck and have decided they disdain the company that misery supplies.

Life coaching also offers tools for people to take responsibility for their lives, for then and only then, is true measurable and sustainable change attained. Our shirking from following wholeheartedly in the Lord's path only confirmed after repeated failures of self-effort and seeking, that His ways were the best all along. Life coaching either through reading on the subject or through an actual licensed life coach is refusal to say no to any aspect of life that is a part of our dreams and goals for our present as well as the future. It is an equipping to give us the courage to conquer our fears and venture into all that we want to be. It always takes prayer for us to arrive at the place where we can accept positive reinforcement and receive some supernatural momentum or spiritual leverage that Valorie mentions in her book. This is necessary to make the focused and fruitful progress that we need in our lives.

Many of us who have hit the halfway mark in our lives are ready to make some huge changes. This could entail resuscitating lost or hidden dreams that we never thought would materialize or manifest. With people living longer because of the growth in technological gains, eating better, exercising more and better mental attitudes due to educational and spiritual gains, it is important to reassess our lives and ask ourselves what haven't we achieved yet that we would like to, what kind of breakthroughs do we want to make in our relationships, how do we want to draw closer to the Lord, and many more. Perhaps we are identifying emotional and spiritual hunger in our lives that needs to be satiated and we are bolstered with the conviction that it can happen.

Certainly, personal maturity and following through on God-given assignments are factors that either propel or impede progress. Maybe other people that directly affected you needed to be in a place that was mutually beneficial or perhaps they were a link to the next step you were to take and they needed to get into position. Other people's healing of all sorts needed to happen as well as some that you had to experience too. Believing there is a timing in everything is certainly helpful when combating stress due to thinking "I missed my destiny', "I'm too old, too young, too fat, too skinny, too educated, …" do you see a pattern here? There will always be excuses we can find until we take action to negate all the lies that the enemy of our souls and sometimes others might whisper to us.

The Life Coaching Craze simply brings all of our dreams into sharp focus and says it is possible to climb that mountain you have never climbed, driven that race car or ridden that race horse (for the animal lovers), painted that masterpiece, written your memoirs, and so forth. This could be real or simply metaphors for that person you want to be. What is stopping you?

Life Coaching could be just the next cog in the wheel that can revolve you into an ongoing forward motion that will gain momentum and move you towards all that has been in your heart. As Julia Child, famed American chef, author and television personality who introduced French cuisine to the American palate through cookbooks and television programs said, “Bon appetit.”

Have a good if not a great appetite for the adventures of discovering what you really want to do with your life and proceed with all the fortitude that is within you. You will also be astounded that you will have an appetite for even more adventure in living since we can never exhaust the depths of potential that the Lord has designed for His people.

CHAPTER 25 – THE LIFE COACHING CRAZE

1. Based on what this chapter presents, where are traumatic areas in your life that need resolution?

2. Are there particular life areas in your career, ministry, relationship or finances where life coaching could help? What is your mission statement?

3. Where do you tend to sabotage your efforts? How can you start to dismantle this negative tendency?

4. What adventures are beckoning to you? Do you have a one year plan for these dreams, three year plan and five year plan? Create one now.

CHAPTER 26 - SPIRITUAL WARFARE IN THE 21st CENTURY

We live in a technological society, knowledge explodes at an exponential level, and we seem to be able to accomplish so much with a click on the computer, iPad, social networking, iPhones, and all the detailed technological apparatuses in between. We seem to really have it made.

In fact, in countries like Japan, robotic servants are being employed to replace their human counterparts. Many jobs are being phased out such as bank tellers, file clerks, cashiers, and similar positions because of our vast storehouse of technology. How does God fit into this morass of technological overload? I believe people are finding themselves in various categories in order to compensate for this welcome or unwelcome intrusion upon our lives.

Having so much technological software at our disposal through which we can research any subject of our choosing and find a plethora of resources can give us the mirage that we are invincible. Anything we want to learn, we can through our computer interactions, tele-conferences and webinars. We can start feeling like we are semi-experts if not the real thing through our knowledge of what is out there on Youtube, Facebook, and Twitter.

Morally speaking, we have changed the rules of order the Bible has so classically and clearly laid out for our perusal, meditation and implementation. Many universal sins or taboos which many cultures other than our Judeo-Christian one, would decry are becoming universally expunged and replaced with "that was how the ancient culture perceived matters" and we are now "enlightened" in our understanding so we can be more accepting.

That may sound good and even fair, but is it truly right? Herein lies one of the difficulties we are facing in our world today. As Christian core values are being metaphorically decapitated, it is not a problem then to throw root causes and their corresponding foundational tributaries or the carcass under the bus. The much-used cliché, out of sight, out of mind, certainly fits the situation in question. The most shocking aspect of this dishevelment of values is that orthodox scholars, pastors and prominent Christian speakers and writers are falling prey to this disarray.

Martin Luther once said in the university that if students attended without a knowledge and respect for God and His precepts or Word, we would have nothing but educated devils. In fact, the Bible speaks of paying heed to lying spirits and doctrines of demons. It seems one of the reasons many are falling prey to this travesty is the enemy, satan, is very sophisticated in our society. He dresses up in a three-piece suit, is educated, knows scripture, gives mental assent to scripture, is multi-talented and knows how to use the parable of the ten talents to his advantage.

It bears fruit all right, but it is the wrong type of fruit and once again we run into a roadblock. As long as the culture values the fruit, this is all that matters. Our values have become skewed. In some cases they are non-existent and this suits many people just fine. They don't even know there is such a thing as spiritual warfare between good and bad. Those are passé distinctions that don't apply to our lives anymore. Do we have a problem or what?

You couple this line of thinking and our technological know-how and you have built a case against the need for the Judeo-Christian God. That spiritual God-shaped vacuum Blaise Pascal speaks of has been filled by our own mental inventions and devices. We think we are pretty clever at this stratagem and we tell ourselves we are removing the need for accountability before God and His final judgment of our lives.

Where does this dichotomy in our culture leave us? Namely, I am talking about those of us who want to adhere to Judeo-Christian principles and rudiments and those who are rewriting what has been even universally acclaimed as sacred. To survive in our culture, we need to have a modicum of technological know-how to make any progress at all. However, boundaries need to be erected when technology attempts to take over our lives and precludes any need for a loving, beneficent God Who desires relationship with us and to fill us with His knowledge which leads us to an eternal assessment of our lives in addition to direction and guidance He wants to give us for this life. Technology, in other words, cannot be the ultimate answer for our souls crying out for satisfaction and fulfillment.

Jesus told the Samaritan woman at the well, "I will give you water from which you will never thirst again." That caught her attention to which extent she asked where she could obtain that water. At that point, she forgot about her own mundane chores and temporarily her shame as an ethically and morally despised woman. Jesus had struck a chord with her. In the course of her conversation with Jesus, she perceives he is a prophet because he tells her she has been married five times and the man she is now living with is not her husband. She is drawn by that knowledge and more importantly, He does not condemn her. At this point, she does not want to hash details out with him or have a deep theological discussion. She wants her deepest longings to be assuaged.

Can technology do this? I assert it cannot and there are those in the ranks of using technology for their life's work or plainly as a lifestyle, that are dissatisfied as this Samaritan woman was with her state and want something more than what they can see, hear or touch with their physical eyes. They want something that is lasting beyond this life and somehow their childlike wonder and hopefulness has not been tainted by the corruption of this world.

These are those who are candidates for the winds of revival sweeping through our country and our world today. They have not shut their minds and hearts to what Romans 1 tells us about, that God is made manifest through His creation. There is such a longing of the heart no amount of knowledge satisfies, but instead supernatural knowledge can.

Because of the intensity of this dissatisfaction of what the world can offer, there will be a corresponding passionate response to the call of God on their hearts. The result will be the Lord can use these technological skills combined with strong faith to make a significant difference in this culture that has come to so many impasses, dead-ends, and moral confusion.

Is this still possible today? While a Christian witness still remains in our world, the answer is a resounding YES! Romans 5:20 says where sin abounds, grace abounds more. As our culture darkens, those who are seeking with their whole heart God's truth will find it. We have His word on it and also as the Scripture says, God is not a man that He should lie. It is time for a personal and corporate turning from sin and as 2 Chronicles 7:14 (NIV) points out, "If my people who are called by my name will humble themselves and pray and seek my face and turn from their wicked ways, then I will hear from heaven, and will forgive them and will heal their land." God's Word never grows old because it is the eternal truth and when we have tasted and seen that the Lord is good, found in Psalms 34:8, then we can truly say the proof is in the pudding.

All's not lost but the battle lines are being drawn. As Isaiah 53:1 asks, "Who has believed our report?" The report of the Lord is positive, redemptive and eternal and so it behooves us to believe His report and not the naysayers.

Are we teachable in this hour in which we live? Will we follow the leading of the Holy Spirit? We are given a choice and are admonished to choose this day who we will serve. As a Bob Dylan song indicates, "You're going to serve somebody." Let us not be deceived and follow the wrong master. Finally, the "battle is not ours, but it is God's", 2 Chronicles 20:15, and He promises to fight our battles for us as we trust Him to follow through on His life-giving promises. This can be the most glorious time for the believer. Let us join arms together!

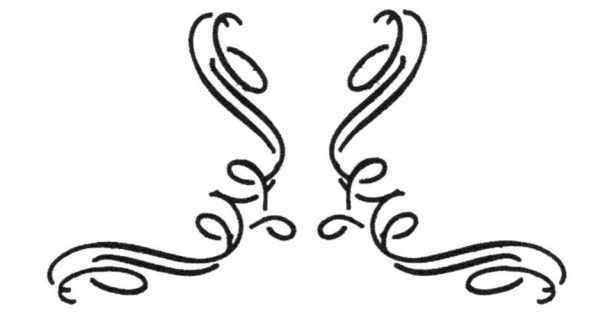

CHAPTER 26- SPIRITUAL WARFARE IN THE 21st CENTURY

1. Where has technology been a help to you and where has it been a hindrance?

2. Have you noticed any other occupation than what is mentioned in the chapter being phased out by technology? What might be some alternatives to these occupations? How is the Lord leading in creative ways to new types of careers?

3. Name two or three values that have been discarded in our culture today. What is the world's reason for doing this and give scriptural reasons for the Lord instilling the values you have mentioned.

4. Name a couple of times satan has deceived you by appearing as an angel of light or dressed in a three piece suit.

5. Where can you find something in common with an unbeliever in order to build a bridge with her or him? What scriptural insight can you give that person?

6. What spiritual battle are you waging? How can you humble yourself in the midst of this battle? What area of warfare are you being led into in order to bring victory into this scenario?

CHAPTER 27 – SOAKING MUSIC

This form of prayer and music has truly become two of the greatest joys in my life. Like anything good and helpful, it is subject to much scrutiny, can be misconstrued and dismantled in its importance and great benefits.

For those of you who are already acquainted with this style of music and prayer, you most likely would attest to the spiritual therapy it is. Soaking prayer music can be characterized as hearing a melodic piece of music often repeated for its soothing quality.

This type of atmosphere is one like the verse James 4:8-9 espouses. It says in the Amplified, "Come close to God and He will come close to you ...as you draw near to God, be deeply penitent and grieve, even weep over your disloyalty..." There is a beckoning, a drawing that one feels with this style of music.

Some of the criticism that is leveled at this genre of music is the type of reactions it evokes. One such criticism is that these reactions, such as, laughter, shaking, rolling, roaring are not mentioned in the New Testament as gifts (Romans 12:6-9, I Corinthians 14:1-6), or fruit of the Spirit (Galatians 6:22-23).

Right away, I beg to differ when it comes to laughter. In Romans 12:8b, we are told a member of the body of Christ is, "he who does acts of mercy, with genuine cheerfulness and joyful eagerness." What accompanies joy most often is the expression of laughter. Of course, the Old Testament is replete with references to laughter. In Psalms 126:2a, it says, "our mouths were filled with laughter and our tongues with singing". Proverbs 17:22 is a celebration; "A merry heart doeth

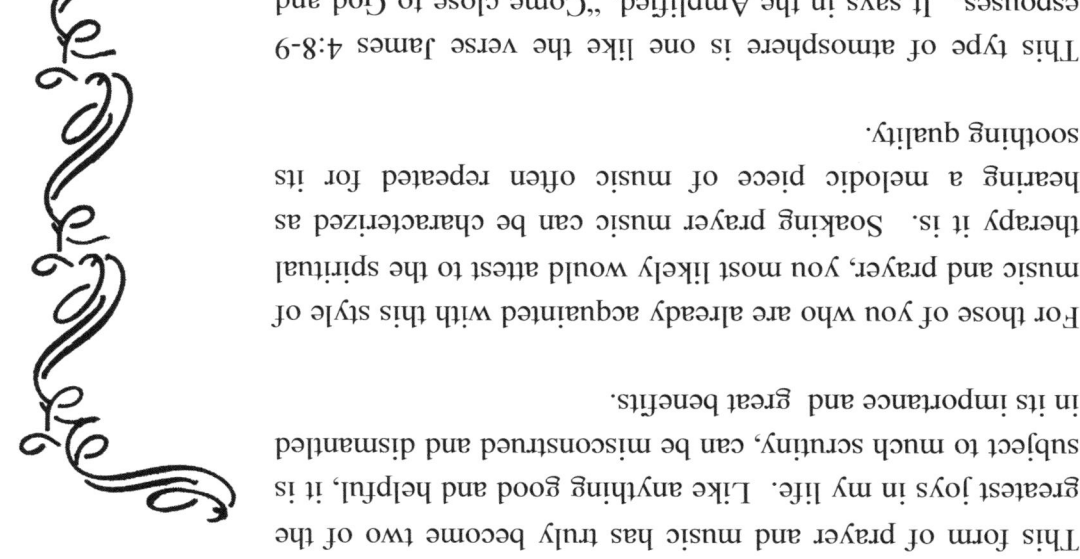

good like a medicine." Another very good reference in the New Testament is from Luke 6:21 in the Amplified and proclaims, "Blessed (happy – with life-joy and satisfaction in God's favor and salvation, apart from your outward condition – and to be envied) are you who hunger and seek with eager desire now, for you shall be filled and completely satisfied. Blessed (happy – with life-joy and satisfaction in God's favor and salvation, apart from your outward condition – and to be envied) are you who weep and sob now, for you shall laugh." This last verse in particular is an obvious indicator that it is the Lord's desire we be filled with joy and laughter.

In Psalm 77:18 (Bible in Basic English) as far as rolling is concerned, we are told, "The voice of your thunder went rolling on; the world was flaming with the light of the storm, the earth was shaking." When one of the reactions is visibly being shaken or rolling even on the floor because of the ministry of prayer or music, there are burdens being lifted and a lightness that is often felt. That which remains is what the Lord has been able to impart to the person who is seeking Him.

Roaring is also akin to shouting and we find many examples of this in the Bible. In fact, shouting is mentioned 72 times in the Bible and laughter is mentioned approximately 23 times in the Bible. Roaring is mentioned in both Joel and Amos. In Joel 3:16, "The Lord shall roar out of Zion, and utter his voice from Jerusalem; and the heavens and the earth shall shake: but the Lord will be the hope of his people, and the strength of the children of Israel." In Amos 2:1, "And he said, the Lord will roar from Zion, and utter his voice from Jerusalem…" Since the word roaring is not mentioned in the New Testament, does the fact it is mentioned at least twice in the Old Testament disqualify this characteristic as being legitimate?

As I have understood the Word of God, the Old Testament has not been abolished; the New Testament only fulfilled its

precepts and teachings. In fact, according to Hebrews 8:6 (Amplified), "But as it now is, He (Christ) has acquired a (priestly) ministry which is as much superior and more excellent (than the old) as the covenant (the agreement) of which He is the Mediator (the Arbiter, Agent) is superior and more excellent, (because) it is enacted and rests upon more important (sublime, higher and nobler) promises."

If in the Old Testament we see the characteristics of laughing, shaking, rolling, and roaring, it certainly appears to be the prerogative of the Lord to roar in Joel 3:16; then these characteristics that the Lord exemplifies to us, His children, should be emulated.

Another one of the criticisms is that an empty space is being created by the participant and in so doing, this can create a place for the enemy to inhabit such as happens in New Age or Eastern religion practices. First of all, if other religions are using soothing music erroneously and not giving glory to the Lord, it only indicates that where there is a counterfeit, a tare if you will, there is the real and the fruit of the real will remain. Psalm 46:10 instructs us, "Be still and know I am God."

Soaking prayer music is soothing and by its nature gives permission to the hearer to meditate correctly on the things of the Lord. New Age practitioners and Eastern religion adherents wrongly use self-centered or idol-centered meditation to assuage their guilt and sorrows since they do not know of our Mediator, Jesus Christ Who has done not only this, but removed our sins as far as the east is from the west (Psalm 103:12).

True meditation on the Lord is supported by many verses in the Psalms particularly as well as others in I Timothy 2:5, Hebrews 9:15, 12:24, Luke 21:14, and I Timothy 4:15. Here are just a couple verses from the psalms. Psalm 104:34 says, "May my meditation be sweet to Him; as for me, I will rejoice in the Lord"

and Psalm 119:97 saying, "O how I love thy law! It is my meditation all the day."

Perhaps at the root of many of these criticisms is the possibility that even Christian people have difficulty with the concept of drawing near to the Lord or embarking on true intimacy with the Lord.

Was this not at the root of the problem with many Pharisees who Jesus rebuked because of their snooty, above it all attitudes when it came to everyone else apart from them? Jesus in Matthew 15:8 reiterates those with similar attitudes in Isaiah 29:13. He says, "These people draw near to me with their mouths, and honor me with their lips; but their heart is far from me, and in vain they worship me teaching as doctrines the commandments of men."

In this teaching, he lays out what is actually going on regarding some of our religious practices. With all our efforts and expertise, we are told that it is in vain if we do not draw close to the Lord with our hearts.

Intimacy, therefore, is a drawing near with our hearts, wanting to be pleasing to God for Who He is. If the result of hearing soaking prayer music causes us to want to be closer to the Lord and bear good fruit in our lives because we want to tell others of our love for Him, I would say this is more powerful medicine than any earthly doctor could prescribe.

In John 4:24, we are told that we are to worship the Lord in spirit and in truth. It seems as Christians we can go on either side of a rut. We either emphasize the Word with hardly any mention of the Holy Spirit and how He operates in our lives, and so can have dull, lifeless, dead worship. Or, we can emphasize the Holy Spirit and experiences we have with Him through His gifts, signs and wonders, and miraculous interventions, but neglect to be centered on the Word bringing substance, clarity, credibility, and true direction to our lives.

We are not to neglect either and make either part an idol or a platform for us to demonstrate our flesh. I believe soaking prayer music has the effect of drawing a person into a deeper study of God's Word and seek the whole counsel in order to be effective for the Lord's kingdom.

First Peter 3:15 (AMP) brings the two elements of worship together in one verse. It says, "But in your hearts set Christ apart as holy (and acknowledge) Him as Lord. (This would support worshipping in spirit.) Always be ready to give a logical defense to anyone who asks you to account for the hope that is in you, but do it courteously and respectfully." (This would support having knowledge of the Word.) When an activity we are engaged in for the Lord brings both these elements together, we should be thankful and praise the Lord for an effective tool for worship. I think soaking prayer music leads a person to this place.

CHAPTER 27 – SOAKING MUSIC

1. Please "Google search" soaking music. Julie True's music is a good pick. Listen for a half hour by lying down or sitting and share what the Holy Spirit shares with you.

2. Have you been filled with holy laughter at a service or Christian meeting? Was it a blessing or hindrance to the service? Please give examples from scripture for either case.

3. Can you identify Pharisaical attitudes in yourself depriving you of the joy the Lord wishes to impart to you? Matthew 7:5 tells us to "remove the plank from our eye so we can see clearly to remove the speck from your brother's eye."

4. What area of your Christian life have you made an idol? What are you neglecting? Can soaking prayer music help to dismantle your idolatry and help you draw closer to the Lord?

CHAPTER 28 -THE GLORY OF GOD

What is the Glory of God and how can His Glory impact us for greater intimacy, communion and fruitfulness for the furtherance of His Kingdom as we live out our lives and callings He us for our destiny?

In Moses' time, the Hebrew children, even though they had witnessed the greatest miracles of any people group in all of history when they were delivered out of Egypt, still had great difficulty coming near to the Lord when they sojourned in the wilderness. According to Exodus 20:18-21, the people witnessed the thundering, the lightning flashes, the sound of the trumpet, and the mountain smoking. When the people saw it, they trembled and stood afar off. Then they said to Moses, "You speak with us, and we will hear; but let not God speak with us, lest we die." And Moses said to the people, "Do not fear; for God has come to test you, and that His fear may be before you, so that you may not sin. "So the people stood afar off, but Moses drew near the thick darkness where God was.

We see here the people were actually repelled by God's glory, but Moses was drawn to it. In the Glory of God, the manifestation and revelation of His love from www.god.net, many helpful nuggets of truth have been pointed out for me that can also relate to where we are today in the body of Christ. There is a distinction that is made between unholy fear and holy fear. The unholy fear causes you to distance yourself from God, but the holy fear causes you to purify yourself and come near to God. When we know God through experiencing His love, intimacy and communion, we will press through our fear into the glory of God's presence. It takes away the fear as First John 4:18 indicates.

Also, since God is a consuming fire (Exodus 24:17), there is something else that happens when we behold God's glory; transformation. This can be both a painful and wonderful experience. When we are consumed, something is being taken away. Prayerfully, it is the dross and chaff that is being removed, but there are things that remain that are being refined and purified. We can turn away from that process because we are afraid to let go of things than cannot withstand the glory of God. We often take our identity from those things that are temporary and not eternal. It is so much better this side of heaven to recognize these things should be dealt with now, so that we can move more directly, confidently and boldly into our new creation reality. Second Corinthians 4:16 tells us, "For our light affliction, which is but for a moment, is working for us a far more exceeding and eternal weight of glory, while we do not look at the things which are seen, but at the things which are not seen."

Something else that God.net addressed for me, is that today we are not much different from the children of Israel in the wilderness. We actually can incur much greater condemnation than they since from Jesus' time on, we have the power of the Holy Spirit and numerous miracles, signs and wonders have appeared from that time to the present. Thank God for Jesus taking all condemnation upon us on the cross so we don't incur the wrath of God upon us.

Today, though, the children of God are still wary of drawing into the supernatural which looks dark and some would even attribute to the enemy because they don't know the distinction between holy and unholy fire. How can this verse be true if we believe wrongly? John 14:12-13 attests, "Most assuredly, I say to you, he who believes in me, the works that I do he will do also; and greater works than these he will do, because I go to My Father. And whatever you ask in My name that I will do, that the Father may be glorified in the Son." What are those greater works? When the kingdom of God is mentioned, these greater works are to heal the sick, cleanse the lepers, raise the dead and cast out demons.

We need not be quick to judge miracles to be the power of evil and not manifestations of God's love. There is a need to be discerning, but it is always to give much more attention on what the Lord is doing on earth, than what we see the enemy doing. Isaiah 60:1-2 reveals that darkness shall cover the earth, and deep darkness on the people, but the Lord will arise over you, and His glory will be seen upon you. We need not have faith in the power of evil, but in the power of God and trusting Him.

Scientifically speaking, the "dark matter" and "dark energy" scientists speak of is the unknown substances which make up the universe. Interestingly enough, it is called darkness because it cannot be detected with any scientific instruments, but the substances are known to be there, because there is weight and the effects of it can be seen. It is what Colossians 1:17 refers to when we are told, "He is before all things, and in him all things hold together." Jesus is the upholder and moves all things like gravity and heavenly bodies in the universe.

Glory in the Hebrew *kabod* does mean weight. The weight of His glory is where we do receive manifestations and revelations of the Father's love and power. Glory then reveals compassion or the Hebrew word *rachum*. It is this kind of compassion that moved the Lord to heal when He was here on this earth and what compels us to move in the same character, strength and power as He. His graciousness is also what reveals His justice, another characteristic of love. Everything the Lord does is connected to His character and purposes for our lives which reveals His divine glory.

Transformation is the key and it will take sacrifice. The story of how a caterpillar becomes a butterfly demonstrates this principle. When the caterpillar is tucked away in its cocoon, it actually disintegrates into complete liquid. It is no longer a caterpillar, but it is not yet a butterfly. It completely dies to what it was, but is not yet what it will be. In fact, if you were to prematurely release the caterpillar out of our view of mercy or compassion, we would irreparably damage the transformation process to becoming a butterfly.

God's glory is like this. We are indeed being changed from glory to glory and yet often when we are in that process, we have no idea naturally speaking what is going on. We must trust the Lord's wisdom for that. God's glory will require that we surrender and give up lesser glories to receive all the Lord has for our identity in Him.

How do we see God's glory in our everyday lives? We love the signs and wonders of the Lord, but another way to look at the supernatural is what may not seem as spectacular, but nonetheless, is the reflection of the Lord's touch on our lives. When we become aware of multitudes becoming saved, divorce rates going down, abortion rates dropping, the entertainment industry becoming transformed towards Christian values as well as government, families, education, economy, media and church life, then we will see kingdom values penetrating our lives in a widespread manner. Let's not be like the Hebrew children who were afraid to enter the Presence of God, but instead want to enter boldly into the throne of grace through the blood of Jesus (Hebrews 10:19). This desire can only come as we want to be close to a God Who is full of compassion and mercy towards us. Let us aspire to live in the Shekinah Glory, His cloud of blessing and righteousness, in His ability and not our own.

CHAPTER 28 - THE GLORY OF GOD

1. What is an example of unholy fear in your life and holy fear?

2. What needs to be consumed in your life? Give reasons why it is both painful and wonderful.

3. How has Christ given you a new identity in Him? Enumerate areas of His character operating in you.

4. Has the Lord been able to do some greater works in your life? Give three examples.

5. Give three examples outside of yourself of about what the Lord is doing in the world today.

6. Give three evidences of the Lord's substance in the world that cannot be seen but points to the Lord's existence.

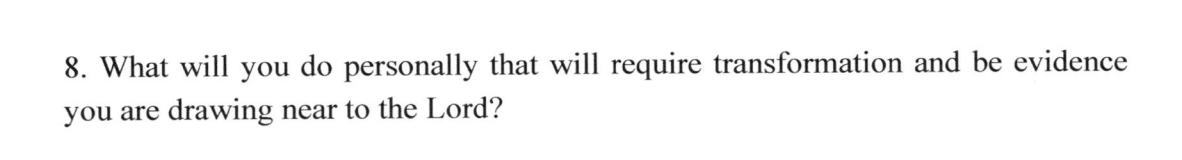

7. Give a biblical example in scripture of the Lord's passion, mercy and justice.

8. What will you do personally that will require transformation and be evidence you are drawing near to the Lord?

CHAPTER 29 - ACT JUSTLY, LOVE MERCY AND WALK HUMBLY WITH YOUR GOD

You may be familiar with these words from Micah 6:8. Earlier in this verse, we are instructed about the fact that the Lord has shown us good and then the question is posed. And what does the Lord require of you? Then we receive the answer which is to act justly, love mercy, and walk humbly with your God. Let's break each of these three answers down and analyze them a bit, shall we?

In Webster's 1828 Dictionary, the definition of justice is as follows: It is the virtue which consists in giving to every one what is his due; practical conformity to the laws and to principles of rectitude in the dealings of men with each other; honesty, and integrity in commerce. Distributive justice belongs to magistrates or rulers, and consisted in distributing to every man that right or equity which the laws and the principles of equity require; or in deciding controversies according to the laws and to principles of equity. This is justice in a broad sense and I believe as much as possible should be adhered to.

A recent article, I read by Johnny Enlow speaking about "2016: A True Year of Jubilee" mentions justice as being a big theme during this year. Transformation is occurring regarding our own justice system which Johnny indicates is "presently highly and inexcusably unjust." He shares the interchangeable scriptures of Matthew 20:16 and Luke 20:16. Both of these share the ideas of justice. In Matthew, the principle of the last being the first and the first will be last is featured. In Luke 20:16, Jesus tells His listeners, the language is a little more stronger because the owner of the vineyard who is the Lord will come and utterly put an end to those tenants and will give the vineyard to others. This is akin to taking away those ministries who is intent is all about them and their agendas, but need to see it is about the Lord's vineyard and not theirs. In other words, it will be a time of promoting and demoting. I am interested in the Lord's justice and want to get in line for the Lord's promotion; how about you?

Loving mercy is not just a New Testament idea as evidenced by this scripture in the Old Testament. However; not until Jesus came on the scene, was mercy personified in a person and on such a large scale which included healing of all kinds of diseases as well as some incurable ones, breaking down animosity between people and gender groups, and emphasizing that we not do our acts of mercy to be seen by men, but to be a matter of the heart to be seen by God. Jesus challenged those regarded as the exemplars of the law, the Pharisees, not to love material things such as the temple or the traditions of men, also an outward act, but to truly love God's mercy and to be moved by compassion. This is a big part of what Jesus was criticized for since He would heal on the Sabbath, feel healing virtue leave his body when a woman pressed through the crowd to touch the hem of His garment, socialize with sinners or the cultural riffraff of His day, meet and transform the life a Samaritan (who the Jews had no dealing with) woman, or refuse to quiet the little children who would cry, "Hosanna, to the Son of David." He demonstrated mercy and was not interested in playing pharisaical games. True heartfelt mercy is what truly changed the people then and now and bring them to the place where they would choose to become a new creation in Christ Jesus.

Walking humbly with your God is the result of acting justly and loving mercy. Since the flesh or self life is mercilessly eradicated when endeavoring to follow these godly mandates, there is a greater opportunity for spiritual success. How does one walk humbly with God? Moses was called the meekest and humblest man on the face of the earth. How did this come about? We know after finding out he was a Hebrew and saw the injustice of his people, he acted rashly and killed an Egyptian, abusing one of his countrymen. He then ran for his life in the desert and wilderness. Even though he did marry and have sons, he spent the next 40 years being a humble shepherd after being the "Prince of Egypt" for the first 40 years. To the Egyptians, this was the most lowly occupation he could have. However, he must have learned so much in God's bootcamp and training process. He learned how to tenderly care for stubborn, foolish sheep, protect and deliver them from predators; he learned patience and weathering hardships through his monotonous shepherding. We don't know what his attitude was truly at that time, but he was indeed in training to become the Lord's great deliverer of the Hebrew people from the nation of Egypt and its Pharaoh. After the burning bush experience, Moses had a more intimate relationship with the Lord than before, and undoubtedly, learned how to hear God more closely and then because of the immense trust and communion he had with the Lord, knew to act on the Lord's instructions to him. In short, Moses did not procrastinate and followed through instead. As James said in James 1:25, Moses demonstrated that in looking into the perfect law, freedom was given and then continuing in it, was not a forgetful hearer, but became an effective doer.

Humility, then, is not the absence of action, but is the result of the right attitude.

CHAPTER 29 - ACT JUSTLY, LOVE MERCY AND WALK HUMBLY WITH YOUR GOD

1. What is justice to you? Name a couple of ways it could be practically applied.

2. What promotion are you looking forward to and what demotion would you prefer to avoid?

3. What are a couple of opportunities you have had recently to show mercy?

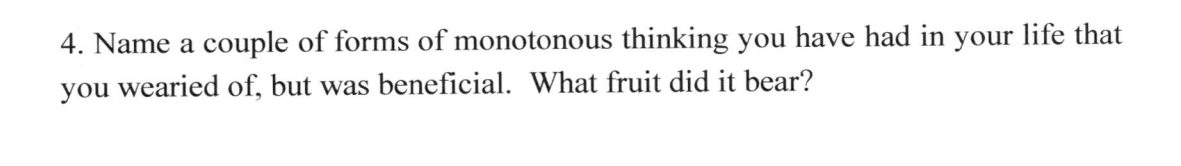

4. Name a couple of forms of monotonous thinking you have had in your life that you wearied of, but was beneficial. What fruit did it bear?

5. What have you been tempted to have pride in? How can you give it over to the Lord and receive His humility instead? What would this look like in your life?

CHAPTER 30 - LADIES AND GENTLEMEN IN WAITING

What are you waiting for? Psalm 37:7 gives us some excellent strategy for waiting. The first thing we are told is we need to be still before the Lord. In this day of age, that is a difficult criteria to lay hold of and actually perform. I want to offer a few definitions of the word still I have found in Noah Webster's 1828 dictionary. It is a favorite of mine because it is based on Judeo-Christian principles. Here they are. The word still can mean: to stop, as motion or agitation, to check or restrain, to make quiet, ceasing or freedom of noise, to calm, become motionless. All of these actions in the natural can seem very forbidding, daunting, even impossible to imagine let alone do. However, this is exactly the attitude where we must go if we are to successfully wait before the Lord. Perhaps it can be likened to someone in the army who is being trained to stand at attention, be quick to hear the commander's instructions, and then when given the release, will carry out the mandate.

The angels are before the Lord continually and their response is "Holy, holy, holy is the Lord, God of Hosts." This declaration can be documented in both the Old and New Testaments. In Isaiah 6:3, the angels call to one another, "Holy, holy, holy, is the Lord God Almighty; the whole earth is full of his glory." It would seem in the New Testament reference to this call, the attitude of being still connotes a type of activity. In Revelation 4:8, the four living creatures, do not rest day or night, saying, "Holy, holy, holy, Lord God Almighty, Who was and is and is to come!" What we may be able to perceive is that our natural inclinations need to be still, but we are alive in our spirits and should be continually aware of the Spirit's interaction with us. It has been said the angels who behold the Lord in ongoing intensity see another facet of His character every time they utter the word holy.

If becoming still before the Lord can give us those types of results and blessing, then it is certainly worth however amount of natural waiting in which we find ourselves enmeshed. By beholding the Lord's character in these times, may give us the answers to questions about God's will for our lives, our healing, connections, prosperity, or our loving actions towards others. It would certainly take away our human tendencies to be agitated, restless, disturbed, anxious, discouraged and the like. We are in a much better position to be full of the joy of the Lord and be able to do His exploits at the appointed time, when we take the time to cultivate an atmosphere of deep trust, worship, and adoration towards Him.

When we are still, then we can be patient. What does the sage Webster's 1828 dictionary have to say about this word? Being patient is having the quality of enduring evils without murmuring or fretfulness, sustaining afflictions of body or mind with fortitude, calmness or Christian submission to the divine will. It is not easily provoked, calm under the sufferance of injuries or offenses, not revengeful. Patience is persevering, constant in pursuit or exertion, calmly diligent. It is not hasty, not over eager or impetuous, waiting or expecting with calmness or without discontent. Amazing! In the definition of this word patience, is the encapsulated meaning of the word wait. By being still and patient, we can also meditate on all this means and endeavor to carry out these character mandates. By crucifying the flesh in this way, we are in a much better position to hear the Lord's voice and know His leading. We can also more easily identify evil, discover traps and then avoid falling into them. We know not to be so easily led by our faulty emotions, that unless, led by the power of the Holy Spirit can lead us hopelessly and helplessly astray. Finally, we are in a posture of knowing when discontent or murmuring tries to arise. We can then make the decision to subdue and muzzle it and give it over to the Lord on the altar of sacrifice. By the way, this will result in transformation of the soul.

In Psalm 37:7 we are also told not to fret. This meaning is variegated as well. To fret can mean to impair, wear away, to agitate, to disturb, make rough, cause to ripple, to tease or irritate, vex, make angry, chafe, to be in violent commotion, to utter peevish expressions. Do you see the beautiful progression this verse affords? When we are still, we are in a better position to be patient. When we are patient, we will identify fretting to be one of those evil traps. None of the definitions of fret that I just mentioned are goals to attain, but instead they are detriments to be discarded. Yet our society as a whole and as individuals are replete with these kind of negative behaviors. The worst fruit of fretting is that it can create unholy desires and then these can lead to strongholds of the mind. We then need to pray to the Lord to remove even the desire to act in this way. This will probably entail the Lord uprooting attitudes such as self-justification if we think we have a right to these mindsets. It is optimum to recognize these attitudes do not bring godly, heavenly fruit that benefits us and all those around us.

The other part of this instruction not to fret, is particularly when we see people succeed in their ways. Really for the first time, I saw this verse is about people succeeding in their ways and not the Lord's ways. Hebrews 11:25 indicates that Moses chose to be mistreated along with the people of God rather than to enjoy the fleeting pleasures of sin. There is no timetable on this. Sometimes people living in a pattern of sin which looks like there are no repercussions to it, may seemingly look like they are prospering for years or for a whole lifetime. Psalm 24:20 makes it very clear. The evildoer has no future hope, and the lamp of the wicked will be snuffed out. When identifying this truth, it helps us then abide by the guidance of not fretting when someone is succeeding in their ways. We want to succeed in God's ways, and be rewarded righteously and not for wicked doings.

The last part of this statement of those succeeding in their ways truly is transparent about what ways are. They are wicked schemes. A scheme is a plan; a combination of things connected and adjusted by design; a system, a project, a contrivance. If a plan is given over to the Lord such as in Proverbs 16:9 in which it is stated, "A man's heart plans his way, but the Lord orders or directs his steps," then that person's plans can and will be established in the Lord. In wicked schemes, a person does not want the Lord's direction and so reaps a wicked outcome.

Taking all of these directives together, I believe, does put us, ladies and gentlemen, in waiting, on a better footing. It is not as if we are waiting in a vacuum with nothing of substance to hold on to. We are given vision in this one scripture alone to make our path straighter and clearer. With this kind of vision, we can reap abundant fruit and joy, that can open doors of favor, connection, promotion, and peace.

No matter the magnitude of the object you are waiting to see come to pass, through the Lord's strategies and guidance, you will reap a tremendous reward, if you faint not. Waiting according to the flesh is not enjoyable, but when we have a vision that has been cast, such as in Psalm 37:7, we will not perish, but can progress in our spiritual walk. This yields great dividends and as Hebrews 10:35 states, we are not to throw away our confidence, because it will be richly rewarded.

This gives a whole new perspective to the inaction naturally speaking and the action of the spirit when we are waiting. My prayer for you is for you to learn the lesson in waiting, get out of some wilderness thinking, and be changed into the next glory of promotion in the Lord. Wear your godly badge of ladies and gentlemen in waiting in humility, but also with great expectation. It is what

equips you for the next glorious season in your life!

CHAPTER 30 - LADIES AND GENTLEMEN IN WAITING

1. What areas in your life disrupt your peace and composure, your stillness? Can they be removed from your life? In what way could an attitude or action of stillness replace them?

2. What words or directives has God given you during times of stillness?

3. Can you give a couple of examples of patience transforming your soul?

4. What are a couple of temptations of fretting in your life? How can you turn this around and bless the persons or circumstances which could provoke the fretting?

5. Name a couple examples in history where a wicked scheme seemed to be succeeding (e.g. Hitler's concentration camps).

6. Do you have a better perspective on waiting and if so how can you apply this to your life?

CHAPTER 31 - WELCOME ME (THE LORD) DILIGENTLY INTO YOUR LIFE

The word welcome is often used interchangeably with the word receive. Let's look at a few verses in which one could easily see the word welcome used. Matthew 10:40 shares, "He who receives you, receives Me, and he who receives Me receives Him who sent me. John 13:20 communicates, "Truly, truly, I say to you, he who receives whomever I send receives me; and he who receives Me receives Him who sent Me." Matthew 18:5 reminds us as we are receiving a little child in Christ's name, we are receiving Him. A very strong admonition to welcoming Christ into our lives is from Matthew 25:35-37 reminding us how important it is to welcome those who are hungry, thirsty, who are strangers, who need clothing, who are sick, and who are in prison. In so doing, we are welcoming the Lord into our midst and our lives.

Shouldn't this be a major and essential pursuit in our lives? Why then do we so often seek other pursuits? It may be no easier than saying we have a lack of trust, lack of knowledge, and a lack of follow through. Let's look at each of these topics separately.

Lack of trust is certainly a major stronghold barrier to having an appropriate welcoming attitude and disposition towards our Lord. What kind of host would we be if we lacked in hospitality, essentially uprooting the welcome mat from our door's threshold? For that matter, what kind of guest are we if are unable or unwilling to receive the host's hospitality because we didn't trust the host's intentions towards us? What if we felt we were being used by the host, gaining nothing in return and that is why we withdraw a godly attitude we may otherwise

have owned? Trusting in the Lord is what enables us to partake in the desires of our hearts. It is through trust we reap the blessings of relationship with the Lord. In Revelation 3:20, Jesus is the one knocking on our door. He demonstrates a patient even trusting attitude towards us that as we hear His voice, we will open the door. In so doing, the Lord can have true communion with us. As a journey of trust ensues, through a continued pattern of welcoming Him, we eventually come to a place where we want Him to be Master or the Host of every part of our lives. He is already the Master, but He waits to be welcomed and asked to enter into our place of residence.

It is incumbent upon the believer in Jesus to grow in knowledge of the Lord and His character, for us to increase our trust in Him. In a recent Joyce Meyer article entitled, "God's Character", she lists three important traits of God's character. The first one is justice which basically means, "God will always make anything that's wrong right." That would certainly be a way to engender trust. Then there is God's goodness. In the article, Psalm 34:8 is featured. This verse shares, "Taste and see that the Lord is good; blessed is the man who takes refuge in Him." Finally, there is holiness. The Greek definition for holy is to be righteous.

God is separate from our ideas or opinions on what is acceptable and commendable. When we recognize that the Lord in all His justice, goodness, and holiness is never wrong, we can grown in trust and love for Him. This type of pursuit certainly aids in cultivating a welcoming attitude towards the Lord in every aspect of our lives. It helps give us confidence that we cannot go astray when we welcome the Lord abundantly to lead and direct our lives.

What about follow through? This is one I frankly have trouble with, not that I don't take action, but often I am going in a lot of directions. I have tried to narrow it down to like-minded kinds of pursuits, which is a help, but still sometimes the total completion and diligent follow through of a task can be thwarted because of this mindset.

A modern definition of follow through is to press on in an activity or process especially to a conclusion. I like adhering to Webster's 1828 dictionary and since there wasn't a phrase such as follow through at that time, I have selected the word completion to define. Completion means to finish, to end, to perfect, to fill, to accomplish.

Most assuredly, we can trust and grow in knowledge of our Savior when Paul shares with us in Philippians 1:6, "being confident of this, that he who began a good work in you, will carry it on to completion until the day of Christ Jesus." Knowing and believing a promise such as this encapsulates the three ways to come near to the Lord who welcomes us to abide with Him. This verse is also a wonderful way to be consistent in a gracious, hospitable, and loving attitude towards our Lord and others. It is a surefire way to grow in grace and to overcome all pretender distractions. It is only the Lord Who can deliver what He asserts and lays out in His Word for us. Why would we ever want anything less?

We must practice coming to Him regularly as the welcoming Host He is and love His Presence better than life itself. In reality, He is our Life. Psalm 63:3 indicates this truth by stating, "Because your love is better than life, my lips will glorify or praise you." When we do this, we are more able to spot the tares in our lives, and allow the Lord to uproot what is not of Him. It is when we think we can do it, we are headed for trouble. Strongholds can be created in our mind also if mistakenly we believe we have a better idea than the Lord. It is then when we recognize the Lord's gentle, yet illuminated presence in our lives, that we can more easily follow Him with great joy knowing He will never disappoint us.

Do you want to have more of His welcoming demeanor in your life? It is yours for the asking, taking and abiding. Let Him remove the hurtful rocks, thorns, and

suffocating cares of this world from you and you will know His peace, joy and love without measure. He is well able and is abundantly desirous of overflowing us with His blessings and treasures. Let us not waste another minute in thinking anyone or anything can satisfy us other than His welcoming Presence, welcoming Him with a renewed understanding of His character. It is communion and fellowship with Him that is His true will for our lives. When we are engaged in His Presence, we can then believe more freely for all that He has in store for us. Let Him be the guest in your house as well as its Host and Master in your life today.

CHAPTER 31 - WELCOME ME (THE LORD) DILIGENTLY INTO YOUR LIFE

1. How have you welcomed the Lord in the manner of Matthew 25:26-37? Give two examples.

2. Where haven't you welcomed the Lord in your life? Would you like to change your decision? How would it make a difference in the areas you have not allowed Him access?

3. What are a couple of mindsets that the Lord is wanting to change in you that interrupt your ability to follow through?

4. What are a couple pretender distractions in your life that can thwart you from God's Presence?

5. Name two to three ways you can practically practice God's Presence in your life.

CHAPTER 32 - LIVING A LIFE OF FORGIVENESS IS LIVING IN THE CONCEPT OF THE JET STREAM

What is a jet stream? They are relatively narrow bands of strong wind in the upper levels of the atmosphere. The winds blow from west to east in jet streams, but the flow often shifts to the north and south. They also form at the boundaries of adjacent air masses with significant differences in temperature such as the polar region and the warmer air to the south. (Intellicast - Jet Streams in the United States) They are fast flowing and typically have a meandering shape. They can start, stop, split into two or more parts, combine into one stream or flow in various directions including the opposite direction of most of the jet. The main commercial relevance of the jet streams is in air travel, as flight time can be dramatically affected by either flying with the flow or against the flow of a jet stream. Turbulence is often found in a jet stream's vicinity, but it does not create a substantial alteration on flight times. (http://en.m.wikipedia.org/wiki/Jet_stream)

This is a basic understanding of jet streams. There is so much more on that subject, but for the purposes of this article, we only need the basics to map out how to successfully walk in forgiveness. We can see how tremendously important jet streams are to navigation. When the navigator can properly interpret the flow of the jet streams, the success of the air flight can be more closely guaranteed. Since we cannot rule out the possibility and in many cases, the probability of turbulence, it is incumbent upon the navigator to adeptly use the jet stream to their advantage. At the very worst, not mastering the flow of jet streams can cause a crash. At the least, mismanagement in corralling jet streams may create a more uncomfortable ride.

What's the relationship with forgiveness? The Lord's atmosphere or jet stream is what we would call the supernatural. Living only in the natural, and ignoring the laws and properties of moving in the supernatural can at the very least cause much frustration, discouragement, and despair. In overriding the sensitivity of impressions or witnesses the Lord gives to us in our spirits, we put ourselves in a very precarious way, resulting in illnesses both physically and emotionally, possibly even incurring death. How can forgiveness stay emotional and spiritual damage in our lives?

Being a person who forgives puts us in the posture of being seated in heavenly places. In gotquestions.org, the Greek word ***epouranios*** means the sphere of spiritual activities. Ephesians 2:6 instructs that God raised us up with Christ and seated us with him in the heavenly realms in Christ Jesus. When we activate forgiveness in our lives, much that would bog us down emotionally, spiritually and physically is removed. What weighs us down and prevents us from moving in a trajectory that keeps us airborne is a result of forgiveness. We need to respond appropriately especially when there is much spiritual turbulence. By responding to negativity with forgiveness, we thwart the enemy's schemes of pulling us down to his level which by the way is not in the same atmosphere as heavenly realms.

In heavenly realms, life is accelerated because it is experienced at a higher level. When there are no restrictions or limitations because God's love is ubiquitous, there is a level of freedom of movement that is incomparable on earth. The closest we can have to that freedom and ease of movement is when we walk in forgiveness. First Peter 5:7 (AMP) demonstrates this truth. We are told to "cast all anxieties, worries, all your concerns, once and for all on Him, for He cares for you affectionately and cares about your watchfully."

If we are not weighed down by the cares of this world and

tune into heavenly sounds and directives, don't you believe we can move more freely, with more anointing, smoothness, and peace in our lives? That's what forgiveness does for us. It's responding in love to every situation, knowing since we have been forgiven from such a great debt, we are free to forgive others. The Lord is able then to guide us speedily, but not hurriedly, to the destination points He has for us each and every day. It is no longer I who live, but Christ Who lives in me. Instead of seeing a demon behind every tree or bush, we see heavenly realms along our pathways. When we are emboldened and strengthened to live life in these heights, we have the capability through living in God's way to deal with any obstacle that is thrown our way.

We are freer also to forgive ourselves for every infraction or sin we might commit, knowing the Lord is greater than that transgression and because He is love, offering us the remedy to deal with our dilemmas. How marvelous to walk in His ways. He has created solutions for every perceived and real issue in our lives. As we respond with forgiveness, we can know the majesty and beauty of living in a spiritual jet stream of unparalleled blessings and joy. Luke 12:32 admonishes us not to be afraid, for your Father has been pleased to give you the kingdom. God's kingdom is all about His lavish forgiveness. He desires us to walk in it and develop a kingdom way of life. Are you weighed down in the natural? Why not come up to the Lord's supernatural, flow in His jet stream and reap an eternity of His blessings for your life?

CHAPTER 32 - LIVING A LIFE OF FORGIVENESS IS LIVING IN THE CONCEPT OF THE JET STREAM

1. Can you give a couple of examples in your life when there has been dire turbulence? How did you respond to it?

2. Can you give a couple of examples when forgiveness helped prevent emotional and spatial damage in your life?

3. Can you give a couple of examples when the Lord speeded aspects of your life up? It could be some unexpected good circumstance, event, healing, or relationship reconciliation.

4. Give a couple of examples how you have been set free from bondages.

5. Name a couple of areas you would like to see the Lord's jet stream working in your life.

CHAPTER 33 - HAVING DIFFICULTY IN RECEIVING LOVE?

Isn't love what we are all seeking for? Why would we have difficulty receiving something we are in hot pursuit of? It seems like we would be the most focused on what love really is such as doing all types of research on the subject. The problem is manifold and in our human condition, we do look for love in all the wrong places.

First of all, we certainly need to look to the Bible for our definition of love. First John 4:8 admonishes us, "Whoever does not love doe not know God, because God is love." First John 3:10 takes it a step further and asserts, "This is how we know who the children of God are and and who the children of the devil are. Anyone who does not do what is right is not God's child, nor is anyone who does not love their brother or sister." Also, I John 4:7 tenderly caresses our emotions, by entreating us in this way: "Dear friends, let us love one another, for love comes from God. Everyone who loves has been born of God and knows God."

We need to believe the Word of God is inspired to believe it is the truth. Second Timothy 3:16 clears up any confusion we might have on that subject. It boldly attests, "All Scripture is God-breathed and is useful for teaching, rebuking, correcting and training in righteousness." Ok, how does this help us understand how to receive love from God?

Since receiving love from God requires an understanding of Him we can gain from Scripture, let's delve into the previous Scripture and look at each of these tools for understanding the character of God.

The importance of correct teaching is seen throughout scripture, but let's look at a few scriptures starting from our earliest knowledge of God's Word.

Deuteronomy 11:18-19 instructs, "Fix these words of mine in your hearts and minds; tie them as symbols on your hand and bind them on your foreheads. Teach them to your children, talking about them when you sit at home and when you walk along the road, when you lie down and when you get up." The teaching of God's Word is primary and is emphasized in every crook and cranny of life.

Matthew 5:19 seriously counsels us about the teaching of God's Word this way. "Therefore anyone who sets aside one of the least of these commands and teaches others accordingly will be called least in the kingdom of heaven, but whoever practices and teaches these commands will be called great in the kingdom of heaven."

Psalms 32:8 lovingly offers, "I will instruct you and teach you in the way you should go; I will counsel you with my loving eye on you." This scripture assumes in a sense we know the Lord is loving, is to be trusted, and we will follow His instructions in the way we should go as well as His counsel.

In addition, two stronger terms, rebuking and correction, are introduced in our knowledge about how to receive love from God.

Proverbs 27:5 shares, "Better is open rebuke than hidden love." Rebuke does have the quality of bringing wrong and hurtful things out in the open. There are scriptures on rebuking all kinds of things. In order to do this, we need accurate and insightful teaching. Some of those scriptures on rebuking are: rebuking a brother, sin, or demonic spirits. Often, rebuking and correcting go together. There is actually a blessing in receiving the rebuke. A few verses in Proverbs proves this point. Proverbs 13:18 tells us, "Whoever heeds reproof is honored," Proverbs 15:5 shares, "He who listens to reproof gains intelligence," (Proverbs 15:32) "love's knowledge," (Proverbs 12:1) "will dwell among the wise and is on the path of life" (Proverbs 10:7). In addition, Proverbs 6:23 reveals "the reproofs of discipline are the way of life."

According to "Embrace the Blessing of Rebuke" in desiringgod.org, "Often it is easier for others in our lives not to say anything, but just let us go merrily on our way down the path of folly and death. But reproof is an act of love, a willingness to own that awkward moment, and perhaps having your counsel thrown back in your face, for the risk of doing someone good. When a spouse or friend or family member or associate rises to the level of such love, we should be profoundly thankful."

Now we are arriving a little closer to what our barriers are to receiving love. If we disregard the Word of God as a safeguard for us in trusting its mandates and instruction are borne out of the unfathomable love of a perfect God, then we have our first severe problem that needs to be rectified. After this is resolved and it will take a lifetime to walk out, then we are on better footing to receive rebuke and correction either when we stumble out of being blindsided by the flesh or the enemy, or out of ignorance or willfulness because at that point we know the Word, but choose to be contrariwise.

It is at this point when we are taught, receive rebuke and correction that we can be trained in righteousness. Let's look at my favorite dictionary, Webster's 1828 Dictionary for a definition. It means purity of heart and rectitude of life; conformity of heart and life to the divine law. It is nearly equivalent to holiness, comprehending holy principles and affections of heart. It includes all we call justice, honesty and virtue.

If what we believe according to God's Word, matches up to sound doctrine, infuses us with an ability to receive loving rebuke and correction, and causes us to believe, think and act in righteousness, we are indeed opening ourselves up to knowing God and receiving His unconditional and perfect love for us.

In a practical way, I want to insert I am increasingly having a better understanding of what a husband's love should be. When I was a newlywed, I knew my husband loved me and I loved him, but what has often been a barrier is my stubborn pride and looking for what could be added to love. I didn't think I was a shameless materialistic person, but in some ways, the way I was raised with so much abundance, motivated me to think that love was great, but it needed addendums. Certainly, one result of the Lord's blessing on one's life is material blessings, but it is only one aspect and should not be the cornerstone of a relationship.

As I have seen the deep love my husband has had for me all these years, through thick and thin, it has made an indelible impression on me. Knowing his love for me is motivated by the Lord, has helped me receive his love and the Lord's in a more profound, deep-seated peaceful way. I have come to recognize the stability, contentment, and consistency he demonstrates reflects the Lord's love and has given me an enhanced perspective on entering through the narrow way.

We can often chafe and wrestle with the Lord about why His encapsulating love often goes against our fleshly grain. What more could we want than have the Lord of the Universe love us with unimaginable tenderness, care, completeness, and beauty?

We don't receive God's love because we still want to do life our way. Prayerfully, as we apply our minds and hearts to understanding and demonstrating the Word in our lives, we are opening ourselves to a higher degree of receptivity. We realize we have everything we need when we have the Lord. This includes first and foremost, the great love He has for us. He wants us to focus on Him and reckon the narrow walk of loving Him is a wonderful journey to embrace, not to shun or be disheartened by. He is the one who will carry us all the way through our lives burden free and cloaked with His inimitable lovingkindness and anointing. All He asks is that we believe Him with our whole hearts, mind and soul. We do this by yielding, adhering to, clinging to, abiding in, and of course, trusting.

Does this mountain of receiving God's love look as insurmountable as previously thought? We have the keys of the kingdom to unlock those blockages and allow God's free flowing love to saturate and touch our lives for all eternity. What a blessing!!!

CHAPTER 33 - HAVING DIFFICULTY IN RECEIVING LOVE?

1. Where have some of the wrong places been towards which you have searched for love?

2. Have you ever questioned God's love for you? What has motivated you to do this? It could be several instances.

3. What are a couple of areas of the Lord's teaching in your life that has enlarged your perception of Him and his will for your life?

4. What are a couple of times where you have been rebuked by the Lord either through His inner witness or through loving reprimands by others? How have you responded to these corrections?

5. In these times where you were rebuked, did you fall into these traps through being blindsided, out of ignorance, or through stubborn willfulness? Has correction helped to set you free so you won't repeat the matter, or are you still going around that same wilderness mountain?

6. Name an example as I did with sharing about my husband when love didn't seem to be enough for you. Have you resolved this issue? Give a couple of scriptures that gives direction for resolution and cite where you have received help for that incorrect mindset.

7. What has the love of the Lord meant for you? Don't hold back in your description of His lavish love. Use scripture, insights, dreams, visions, circumstances, anything that will help enhance your heart knowledge of Him as your eternal Bridegroom.

JUST FOR FUN

CHAPTER 34 - A LOOK AT SOME FUNNY LADIES

What do Lucille Ball, Carol Burnett, and Chonda Pierce have in common? They all have red hair! No, only two do and at least one was not a natural redhead (any guesses?).

They are all living today. No, Lucille passed away in 1989 from heart complications even though her television show "I Love Lucy" is the longest running syndicated series. It has never stopped for that matter since its inception in the early '40's. However, I digress, back to our story.

One stands out truly as a comedic pioneer and paved the way for the others. Lucille played a scatter-brained housewife with the ability to turn simple chores into unparalleled fiascoes. She was clumsy and unsophisticated at nearly everything she tried (which was almost everything) and won the hearts of average Americans across all social and cultural lines. She had a wide range of experiences and talents that made her such a success. She also had been in 43 films and was known as the "Queen of the B Movies" playing a variety of roles such as a nurse, dancer, flower girl or clerk. She played seriously dramatic roles to light hearted romantic leads.

Lucille Ball said that you were either funny or you weren't – in other words you either had it or you didn't. With a pause, a stutter, or a firmly asserted absurdity, she expressed quirky, awkwardness that audiences ate up. She seemed to understand television before it understood itself. Who can believe now that she was once told that she had no future at all as a performer? Who could ever forget

Lucy and Vivian Vance's (another great comedic artist) timing and responses on the " I Love Lucy" Show? My favorite sketch and perhaps for many of you was "Vitameatavegamin" and the slip of the tongue when after many camera shoots (part of the sketch), the supplement having too much alcohol in the ingredients caused Lucy to say "Are you unpoopular?" "Do you poop out at parties?" "Well, all our troubles can be solved in this bittle lottle, this little bottle."

What about the stuffing of the chocolates in Lucy and Vivian's mouths and clothing because the conveyer belt in the candy factory is too fast? Then the supervisor thinks the gals are making great progress so she gives the order to speed up the process and the increased stuffing only increases our laughter as an audience. There are so many comical episodes that we would be here all night, and then some, if I attempted to relate those scenes to you. We found Lucy so very entertaining because she intimately connected with the lives of housewives in the '40's and '50's. The escapades were taken to unusually hilariously exaggerated extremes because Lucy vented the feelings and desires that other women of that time may have only dreamed or thought about. Lucille Ball combined the excitement of vaudeville, the wonder of movies and the intimacy of radio when she came into our homes through television. Lucille Ball and her programs are timeless, though, because we still laugh at her antics today. (en.wikipedia.org/wiki/LucilleBall)

Then we have Carol Burnett. Lucille Ball and Carol Burnett met in 1963. They became fast friends and in fact, Carol was a guest on several of the "Lucy shows" and Ms. Ball even offered Carol her own syndicated sit com which Carol politely declined. Carol instead developed her variety show, but Lucy was indeed her mentor. The friendship was so strong that every year Lucille would send flowers to Carol for her birthday. The day Ball died flowers from her came to Carol with the card saying "Happy Birthday, Kid. Love, Lucy."

Carol Burnett was known not only for her talent, but her love of fans. She never refused signing autographs or refused those wanting to take pictures with her. Originally, she studied at USC, took a degree in journalism, but left it in 1954 to pursue acting. Not surprisingly, she was known as the most bankable singer-actress of the time. Her show had 23 Emmy Awards during its 11 year run. The networks did not want Carol to do a variety show because they thought only men could be successful at variety (and ladies are the ones who can multi-task, go figure). Burnett's contract was that they give her one season of whatever kind she wanted to make and she opted for variety. Remember, the tugging of the ear at the end of her shows. This reportedly was a message for her grandmother who raised her and saw many of the shows that Carol was doing well and loved her. Carol struck a chord with her hilarious sketches such as "Went with the Wind," "As the Stomach Turns" and Mrs. Wiggins and Mr. Tudball. In the latter, Mr. Tudball who is Swedish and so speaks with an accent calls his secretary, Mrs. H-Wiggins. One key phrase here is, "You're the only person I know that can tailgate herself." She keeps putting on nail polish and looking at her nails while Mr. Tudball is talking to her and says, "Got that?", after explaining a simple instruction to her that she usually manages to misinterpret. When she says, "I think so", he says, "That's dynamite" and "the fog is beginning to lift." One final word on Tudball and Wiggins – she's always slow, never answers the intercom and tries to open the door with wet nails – he asks her if she would like a revolving door.

In "Went with the Wind," Rhett played by the late Harvey Korman says to Scarlett about the green dress she makes from the curtains at Tara, her home, "That gown is gorgeous, Scarlett." She says, "I saw it in the window and couldn't resist it." Scarlett later calls Rhett the "Scum of the Ocean", and "Chicken of the Sea".

Carol's show went on for eleven seasons and believe it or not, Tim Conway who was perhaps her funniest cast member was a fixture guest for the first eight seasons before he became a regular staff member.

Some Carol Burnett phrases are: "Comedy is tragedy plus time." "Giving birth is like taking your lower lip and forcing it over your head." "I don't have false teeth. Do you think I'd buy teeth like these?" On a more serious note – "Words, once they are printed, have a life of their own." Another trademark of hers was the Tarzan yell and her red hair. Her mother told her " You can always write, no matter what you look like" which caused Carol great insecurity. (en.wikipedia.org/wiki/Carol_Burnett)

Dubbed "Queen of Clean", Chonda Pierce who is probably the least known of these comediennes to many of you, got her start during a 6-year stint at the theme park in Opryland, USA in Nashville, TN. She impersonated Minnie Pearl, which some of you may recognize by her signature symbol, her hat she always wore with a price tag on it and then saying in a loud voice to everyone, "HOWDY!"

Armed with an abundance of unpretentious Southern charm and laser sharp wit, Chonda has been entertaining audiences for more than a decade. She has used her gift of storytelling and transferred it into a multi-faceted career. Chonda is a member of the Christian Comedy Association and is a spokesperson for World Vision and co-hosted the 2009 Christian Music Hall of Fame awards along with Christian recording artist, David L. Cook (National Christian Recording Artist). She also has won three Emmys for co-hosting "Aspiring Women." Her sketches are like Lucy's and Carol's in that her popularity and reception by audiences is because she relates to them exactly where they are and usually in very everyday events. She draws heavily from her roots as a preacher's kid in South Carolina and uses an arsenal of material that is quite hilarious. She will say that wooden pews and hellfire preaching perhaps did a little damage since she says that's where the warped sense of humor comes from. She attributes though her solid roots to help her to know what to weed out and what to hold on forever. In accordance with this, often there is a Christian bent to her pieces such as the time she took her mother to Niagara Falls for a concert (she sings too) with her while it was snowing and her mother says to her "I hope you are not talking about hell tonight – it's so cold in Niagara Falls, they'd probably want to go." Some of the titles of her sketches are "My Mother and the Mini Bar", "My Mother Scares Me", "Raised in the South", "Menopause Parking", "Weird Things Happen to Me", "Chonda Pierce, this ain't Prettyville" and "Did I say that out Loud?" In "Weird Things Happen To Me," she shares some unusual stalker type scenarios that she may or may not have encountered such as a woman sticking a book and a pen underneath her bathroom stall and saying to her, "Honey, the van is leaving in a minute, would you mind signing this for me?"

In another instance, Chonda arrives early at her hotel room at 7 or 8 AM, which for a night owl is early. The maid says the room is clean and in order, but when she slumps down on the bed, she discovers that she is not alone and anxiously wonders if word got out would her reputation be ruined. She tells the maid that she left something in there. They both go back in and then the maid says, "Ma'am, we have a problem, in which Chonda now sees the true perspective and then says, "No, you have a problem. I wanted stiff sheets not a stiff in the sheets."

Chonda talks more recently about overcoming fears. A relationship with God, she asserts, is how we most fully feel complete. She has also lent her celebrity status to charitable causes such as "Branches Recovery Center" which helps people suffering from depression and other recovery issues. She herself is a survivor of depression. In this short entertainment sketch, I think it is clear to see what has made these women funny and successful is they were willing to take some risks and each one in her own right is a pioneer of some aspect of life and comedy. It is noteworthy there are and were mutual relationships built through the television shows and live concerts between performer and audience that were very real, sincere, and fulfilling. Humor helps form a bonding aspect of relationships from our common experiences for either joy or grief. (en.wikipedia.org/wiki/Chonda_Pierce)

I think Carol Burnett encapsulated what I am trying to say here when at the end of each of her shows after talking to her audience and answering their questions at the beginning of the show and then doing the sketches, she sings:

"I'm so glad we had this time together, just to have a laugh and sing a song, seems we just got started and before we know it comes the time we have to say, so long. So long!"

CHAPTER 35 - OUR FASCINATION WITH BED AND BREAKFAST INNS

We have a fascination for simply the name inn since the time when Jesus was born in Bethlehem over 2000 years ago now.

What does the name inn connote? Most of the time we have warm, cozy impressions of how an inn looks from the exterior as well as interior. Often we enjoy visiting another time in history when life moved a little slower, and let's face it, don't we all love to be pampered?

Bed and Breakfast inns are truly known for this wonderful kind of hospitality as well as offering a time of relaxation for its guests. For the Bed and Breakfast connoisseur or aficionado, the variety of creative culinary delights that one might not find as readily in a cosmopolitan restaurant is sure to bring delight to many.

When one searches the Internet these days, we can find so much information about this subject such as inns can also have the appellations of lodge, cabins, cottages, and guesthouses. They often are situated in amazing settings with panoramic views. You can find these inns in directories or planners nationally and internationally complete with maps. In the directories, you can find inns for sale, innkeeper guidelines and instructions and recipes for innkeepers. With all the organization that is at our fingertips which beckons us to take advantage of hotel package deals, stay in rooms which are fairly similar to each other and utilize the free continental breakfasts in the morning, why do we still insist in breaking away from all of that and yield to the search of the perfect bed and breakfast deals for our particular needs?

I propose that we desire adventure in our sometimes drab, mundane, and uneventful lives and want something unique, creative, and crème de la crème. Within us are deep emotional and spiritual cavities that cannot be satisfied with anything that smacks of the humdrum, routine, and non-romantic. I think that Bed and Breakfast Inns give us the opportunity to explore these paths in our hearts and psyches that could also lead us to our destinies and purposes in life. We tend to live in such compartmentalized, scheduled lives that we seldom have the luxury of dreaming and planning what it is that we really want to do with our lives.

People are often looking for this when they plan for a bed and breakfast escape. In an effort to shed our demarcation points in our lives, people also want to blend all aspects of their lives into one. In our increasingly computerized and technologically oriented world, we search for the experience of combining our work with other aspects of our living such as our recreation, eating, sleeping, relating. We are looking for more continuity and peace in our lifestyles and a bed and breakfast type inn may be just the solution if only for a little while.

Sometimes in the event of staying at bed and breakfast inns, our imaginations really start taking off and we fancy that we too could be an innkeeper and have our own estate to manage and through which show hospitality to strangers. There is such a place that my husband and I have dreamed about that is not just a castle in the sky, but is a real place. It actually is where my father grew up in Pittsburgh and has a real name, "Four Winds." At least, that is the name it had in those years, but may not be known by this name now as it has changed many hands in various sales and purchases.

It stands today as a lovely English Tudor home at what was once the highest point in Pittsburgh, PA. As a child, I had grandiose memories of Easter egg hunts on the three acres of land this house claimed, having homemade warm applesauce, canned pears, reading countless hours in the home's library, playing, exploring, dreaming outside, and remembering Christmas Eves spent at the house. My Nana put the tree up that evening since she had a German background and this is what she did in her household. Nana had a massive garden on the side of the hill in which she labored intensely and collected many slides of her plants and flowers that she featured at her garden club. Her property was also the site of the return of the Monarch butterflies every year about which she also had slides.

It was this backdrop in which my husband and I started to dream build about some day buying Four Winds back and creating our own Bed and Breakfast Inn. The house was built of English sandstone and it was brought directly from England. In my father's growing up years, the family had a maid and she had her own upstairs bedroom near where all the children were. The parents slept downstairs. There was also a sewing room along with the library, a large dining room with closing French doors, and even a "dumb waiter" in the kitchen. Laundry was also thrown down the chute directly under the "dumb waiter". Anything from the basement could be brought upstairs on this contraption! What historic memories I had!

Anyways, Mike's and my thinking was that we could offer this inn as a retreat center for writers, ministries, or even a recovery center for burned out people. I enjoy cooking, so that part did not seem to be too formidable. It is an idea that hasn't waned over time and so perhaps there is still the possibility. When you are a dreamer like me, anything can someday be a reality.

Bed and Breakfast Inns also reflect the personalities of the innkeepers and the historic nature of its surroundings. Just recently, my husband and I traveled to Carthage, MO and stayed at the Grand Avenue Inn. This was of a Victorian nature (which I loved) and the inn itself was noted for its exquisite and peculiarly unique stained glass windows in each of the main rooms downstairs. Because of fires during Civil War times, the homes of the 1840's had been destroyed. This particular inn had been built in 1890 and then was a mansion that was used by those who benefited from the booming mining business that virtually exploded in Carthage at that time. Each of the bedrooms reflected a literary theme such as the Hawthorne room (where we stayed), the Laura Ingalls room and the Mark Twain room. Books by these various authors were situated in those rooms for our reading enjoyment as well as some of the more modern conveniences such as a TV and DVD player. Jacuzzis are becoming more popular in bed and breakfast inns and this Victorian Inn claimed this asset to its benefit as well.

You usually have an opportunity to meet with the other guests at breakfast and this inn was no exception. We met a young honeymooning couple that received their stay at the inn as a gift from the bride's parents. We did not want to overstay our welcome, but Michael and I were cordial and gave a few tips from a "sage" couple celebrating our 32nd anniversary.

One of my personal favorite inns was years ago when I was a college student touring the Lake District situated in northern England. I was studying with my college and one day three of us young ladies took off on a separate tour to William Wordsworth's (the famous English poet) country. Wordsworth published a book called Guide to the Lakes and later was changed to A Guide through the District of the Lakes in North England.

What was immensely intriguing and close to my heart since I was studying literature, was this section of England which attracted many poets and authors. Other poets such as Samuel Coleridge and Robert Southey, a staunch friend of Wordsworth's, actually lived in the Lake District. Many other literary figures including Shelley, Sir Walter Scott, Nathaniel Hawthorne, John Keats, Lord Tennyson, and Thomas Carlyle made numerous visits to the area.

Perhaps one of the most beloved of these figures might be Beatrix Potter, author of the Peter Rabbit book series, who lived in an area called Hill Top Farm. A wonderful movie named MISS POTTER starring Renee Zellweger was made recently and was filmed in this lovely area of England. At that time, though, I only knew what a lovely spot this was and we stayed at an old English Bed and Breakfast Inn. I don't know if it had a name, but the adventure was ingrained deep in my memory. I believe we had down comforters, which is the norm for many of the colder parts of Europe. The breakfast was typical of the area. The bacon was thick and so was the bread. Tea was offered instead of coffee. Since it was in the fall of the year, we appreciated all the creature comforts that contributed to warm, fuzzy feelings.

When it comes down to it, we all like the personalized care and creative touch that Bed and Breakfasts do offer. Through the Bed and Breakfast Finder on the Internet, gift certificates can be purchased, inns are reviewed, recipes are shared, and even the chance of winning a gift certificate is given for doing your own personal review of an inn that you particularly enjoyed. Bed and Breakfast Inns are a reminder when we go the extra mile and take time to be especially conscientious and kind to others, our appreciation factor goes sky high. The time that is taken by the innkeepers to install the little extra touches as well as a comfortable bed, Jacuzzi, the library of books and DVD's, and of course the breakfast does not go by unnoticed by an adoring public. May the traditions of Bed and Breakfast never go out of style.

POSTSCRIPT

I have enjoyed compiling these short articles together for your edification, perusal or simple enjoyment. The Lord is glorified in everything we give to Him through our talents, personalities, careers, associations, and relationships. My prayer is that you have been able to see Him through these "rocks crying out" (according to Luke 19:40) articles. Also, my prayer is He would multiply what you need in a multitude of ways through a word, words, phrases or the entire article or through the questions. He can certainly touch you right where you are and I pray, most importantly, if Jesus is not the Lord of your life, you would simply pray to Him to forgive you from all your sins, thank Him for what He did for you on the cross, dying for your sins, and giving you new eternal life with Him. After all, He is everything you need in this life and the next. May He make this truth real and apparent in your life today and every day! Amen!

https://www.facebook.com/blessedbyhispresence

76842855R00129

Made in the USA
Columbia, SC
17 September 2017